Ac/4003

MENTAL HANDICAP
DILEMMAS OF PARENT-PROFESSIONAL RELATIONS

CROOM HELM SERIES ON SPECIAL EDUCATIONAL
NEEDS: POLICY PRACTICES AND SOCIAL ISSUES

General Editor: Len Barton, Department of Education,
Bristol Polytechnic, Bristol

Special Education and Social Interests
Edited by Len Barton and Sally Tomlinson
Coping with Special Needs: A Guide for New Teachers
Geof Sewell
Redefining Remedial Education
Hazel Bines
Teaching Children with Severe Learning Difficulties: A Radical Reappraisal
Sue Wood and Barbara Shears

MENTAL HANDICAP

Dilemmas of Parent-Professional Relations

Simon Dyson

CROOM HELM
London • New York • Sydney

© 1987 Simon Dyson
Croom Helm Ltd, Provident House, Burrell Row,
Beckenham, Kent, BR3 1AT
Croom Helm Australia, 44-50 Waterloo Road,
North Ryde, 2113, New South Wales

Published in the USA by
Croom Helm
in association with Methuen, Inc.
29 West 35th Street
New York, NY 10001

British Library Cataloguing in Publication Data

Dyson, Simon
    Mental handicap: dilemmas of parent-professional
    relations. — (Croom Helm series on special
    educational needs).
    1. Mentally handicapped children —
    Care — Great Britain 2. Parent and child
    I. Title
    362.3'8'0941   HV901.G7
    ISBN 0-7099-4566-3

Library of Congress Cataloging in Publication Data

ISBN 0-7099-4566-3

Printed and bound in Great Britain
by Billing & Sons Limited, Worcester.

CONTENTS

Acknowledgements
Series Editor's Introduction

1. An Introduction 1

2. The Process of Research 6

3. Practical Difficulties 26

4. Problems with the Services 71

5. Obtaining Information 127

6. An Open Letter to Parents of Mentally-
    handicapped Children 171

7. An Open Letter to Professionals 194

Appendices 1-5 219
Bibliography 226
Index 229

For my brother, Adrian Nicholas Dyson

ACKNOWLEDGEMENTS

I should like to thank all the parents, children and professionals for their kind co-operation in this research, which was funded by the Economic and Social Research Council. This book is based on a thesis submitted to the Department of Sociology, University of Warwick, for a PhD, which was failed by the examiners.

I should like to publicly declare my sincere thanks to my supervisor. Meg Stacey gave me enormous support both as a colleague and as a friend for which I shall always be grateful. I would particularly like to express my admiration for my parents, who alone supported my decision not to compromise my belief that there should be no logical gap between what is written as an attempt to change practice and what is valued as academically worthy. My thanks are due to Roger Burridge who then helped me to argue the case with the University of Warwick for a student's right to appeal. I am also indebted to Len Barton and Will Swann for the faith they showed in my work when my confidence was low. Thank you to Jan Read, David Field and to members of the Warwick University Medical Sociology Workshop (1981-84) for comments on early drafts of the work, and to Hilary Bayliss for typing the initial report to the parents and the professionals of the study. Jan Read also demonstrated to me through her work a powerful way of linking critical insight and practice.

Naturally the support needed to write a book depends on many friends. Syd Holloway, Tim Newburn, John Williams, Tony Lawson and Barry Troyna all helped me find part-time work, or gave up part of their work for

Acknowledgements

me, without which I could not have completed the research. Tony Lawson and John Jackson put up with long periods of my depression with great concern. John also rescued the manuscript from the dustbin and laid the sheets of paper out to dry. This support, together with other important friendships, helped me through the vile insanity of events which dominated the period of my research interviews.

"Sufiya Zinobia Hyder blushed uncontrollably whenever her presence in the world was noticed by others. But she also, I believe, blushed for the world.
(......)
This was the danger of Sufiya Zinobia: that she came to pass, not in any wilderness of basilisks and fiends, but in the heart of the respectable world. And as a result that world made a huge effort of the will to ignore the reality of her, to avoid bringing matters to the point at which she, disorder's avatar, would have to be dealt with, expelled - because her expulsion would have laid bare what-must-on-no-account-be-known, namely the impossible verity that barbarism could grow in cultured soil, that savagery could lie concealed beneath decency's well-pressed shirt. That she was, as her mother had said, the incarnation of their shame. To comprehend Sufiya Zinobia would be to shatter, as if it were a crystal, these people's sense of themselves; and so of course they would not do it, they did not, not for years."

Salman Rushdie, SHAME

SERIES EDITOR'S INTRODUCTION

In academic, popular and official literature a great deal has been written about parent-professional relationships. They are often represented as being fundamentally important and valuable for all the parties involved. A range of platitudes is used to describe such relationships including, 'partnership', 'participation' and 'co-operation'.

Parents are increasingly being involved in primary schools to help listen to children reading, indexing the library books or preparing other resources. Since the 1980 Education Act more parents are now involved in membership of the governing bodies of schools. Also, the 1981 Education Act can be seen as an extension to parents' rights. (Wolfendale 1986)

However, the theme of parent-professional relationships is a contentious one, in that it involves questions of decision-making, choices, priorities, rights and power. Part of the difficulty with such language as 'partnership' is not only its imprecise nature and the ways in which it can mean different things to different groups of people, but also, it is an ideal which is concerned with what could be, or should be, as opposed to what is. Despite all the exhortations it would seem that the realisation of such ideals has hardly been met. Indeed, such rhetoric can be viewed as a 'smoke-screen' that obfuscates the realities of a very different set of conditions and experiences. From a parent's perspective these can be characterised by mistrust, frustration, anger and bewilderment. In the recent Report on 'What LEAs tell Parents under the 1981 Education Act' Rogers (1986), the failure of LEAs to inform parents of their rights or to clarify what the authorities' legal obligations are in their relationship, are documented. It is one thing to change legislation, it is quite another to ensure that it is effectively implemented. Parents suffer as a consequence.

The author of this book is concerned with the unequal power relations between parents and professionals and that professionals' assumptions and practices should be viewed as questionable from a parental perspective. He is committed to encouraging the development of understanding that will contribute to the realisation of change. Part of this task involves an attempt to provide the reader with some insights into the sorts of conditions under which a particular group of parents, at a specific point in history, struggle to bring up their children. Their relationship to various formal services, encounters with professionals, the difficulties of obtaining information and the question of confidential files, are some of the issues considered in the book.

The accounts offered provide us with some much needed understanding of what the process of parent-professional relationships entail. We are given some indication of the sorts of assumptions and practices that characterise some professionals' thinking and behaviour. The writer offers telling glimpses of what it must feel like to be on the receiving end of such a relationship.

This is a disturbing book, which will hopefully provoke the reader into a re-examination of some of the crucial issues which it covers. The question of how we can effectively work towards the democratisation of existing institutions, relationships and practices, is a crucial one. There is no place for complacency because the welfare of children is at stake.

My hope is that this book will contribute towards a more open, informed debate and dialogue between interested parties. More particularly, that rhetoric will be realised in practice and the rights of parents and their children will be respected and protected.

Len Barton

Rogers, R. (1986) Caught in the Act - What LEAs tell Parents under the 1981 Education Act. The Spastics Society.

Wolfendale, S. (1986) 'Involving parents in behaviour management: a whole school approach' in <u>Support for Learning</u>, Vol. 1, No 4, pp 32-8.

Chapter One

AN INTRODUCTION

This study concerns the parents of mentally-handicapped children, and to a lesser extent the various professionals, including academics, who impinge on their lives. However, the study is not intended to be academic, popularist or liberal. There is, for example, no review of the literature in the academic tradition. Neither is there an attempt to bring the subjects of the study to life in a more popularist manner. Lastly, there is no liberal weighing-up of the perspectives of professionals on the one hand, and parents of mentally-handicapped children on the other.

Reviews of the literature are primarily for other academics. Cynically, one might view a literature search as one means of controlling who has access to the publication of their research. Social scientists in particular have been quick to expose 'gatekeeping' and 'rites of initiation' in other professionals, but do not always reflect on their own socially constructed procedures. In this book I criticize a number of procedures of doctors and psychologists as being based on self-protection and self-interest. In my opinion, therefore, to accede to a measure such as a review of the literature, which can similarly be construed as a protectionist measure of the academic professions, would be to systematically undermine my own work. Professionals have the time, space and money to develop ways of being that are not accessible to many of their clients. Professionals have developed as a category of person partly as a separation from the type of work that is a precondition of modern life, such as material production, reproduction of children, housework in the private domain,

1

and clerical, service and administrative tasks in the public domain. Freed from the constraints of what they can then conceptualize as less important or even menial work, professionals may then regard the effects of those same constraints as deficiences in their clients. For example, those parents of mentally-handicapped children who find they have neither the time nor the energy to pursue exercises with their children, assigned to them by speech therapist, physiotherapist or teacher, are regarded as poor or uncaring parents. Professional academics, too, have the time, space and money to engage in procedures such as reviews of literature, which others do not. (As a student I enjoyed some of that time and space.) Now, it might be argued that certain protectionist measures have a beneficial dimension. After all, one would not submit oneself to just anyone to be operated upon. Similarly one might argue that reviews of literature have a value in acknowledging conditions that have been taken up and built upon. Indeed, one might turn the argument back against the author and charge that to reject a review of the literature is to avoid the 'menial work' on which one's writing depends. Therefore, in the following chapters, where I am aware of continuities and departures from previous research, this is acknowledged. Where such continuities and differences are not acknowledged, this is through lack of awareness, and it would be more appropriate for others to comment on how such themes arise independently. I see no purpose in executing badly a review that others are better placed to do. But equally I reject the assumption that this should debar my research from a hearing.

Perhaps, though, I should let the reader have a more personalized insight into the lives of these families of mentally-handicapped children. There are several reasons why this cannot and should not be so. The first concerns the possibility of the professionals of the study identifying which parents have been critical of them. Now this presents a problem. Part of my criticism of professionals is to be that they misuse the notion of confidentiality in order to avoid external evaluation or monitoring of their work. The same criticism might equally be made of this study which presents no detailed elaboration of its subjects. And yet, given any sense of responsibility to the parents of mentally-handicapped children as the subjects of research, I see no easy resolution to the dilemma.

Informal conversation with parents during the course of the research suggested that several would not voice criticisms directly to professionals because they feared (with considerable justification as we shall see) that they would be labelled as troublesome and that their child would be discriminated against. In any case, such personalized portraits of the subjects of the research are beyond reconstruction. All records of the research, except for a written thesis, were destroyed within three years of the first fieldwork (April 1982) consistent with my expressed views on the inappropriate nature of professional records (Dyson, 1986). Furthermore, any such portraits would, I believe, have led to the type of subjective and moralizing prose that is to be criticized in professional files. Finally, the provision of such character descriptions would provide the reader with the opportunity, so often seized by the professional, to engage in a pseudo-psychological analysis of their clients.

The purpose of this study is not to provide a balanced account by presenting the viewpoints of the parents and the perspectives of the professionals each in their turn. Interactionist studies of relations between doctors and clients, such as Stimson and Webb (1975), Strong (1979) and Davis (1982) are not politically unbiased and objective, but demonstrate a liberal bias. In an unequal power relationship it is not neutral to give equal credence to the rhetoric of the relatively powerful as to the relatively weak, for example. One aspect of the problem can be stated as follows. The situation for many of the parents seemed to be that their viewpoint was not considered at all by professionals, or was only considered in a highly selective way, or else was assumed to be a defensive cover-up for their real feelings and problems. It would not, therefore, be a neutral act for a sociologist such as myself to treat what parents say to me at intereview as rhetoric. That would be to replicate those very systems of oppression which characterize their relationships with doctors, psychologists and other professionals. If one takes the contention of Foucault (1979) that power produces a reality from which one can then derive knowledge, then at least three options suggest themselves for research. The researcher might knowingly embrace this power with the result that an ultimately conservative type of knowledge would emerge in which 'everything is as it is' and where no strategy for change

3

is admitted. Or these relations of power over the research subjects are not sufficiently confronted and claims of relative objectivity are made in a knowledge that actually has a liberal bias. Or else, precisely because a political choice of some kind is unavoidable, the researcher can try to put forward the conditions under which what parents of mentally-handicapped children feel and say could be the starting point for a critical response to their situation. The purpose of this book is to attempt to move towards this critical response, not (primarily) to understand why parents, professionals and researcher behave as they do.

Bearing this in mind, Chapter 2 treats my relationship of power over the subjects of my research as problematic, and as a source of data in itself. Chapters 3, 4 and 5 take up issues, which from interviews with the parents seem important to them. It is important that the organization of the book reflects its general concern, namely that professional behaviour should be viewed as problematic from a parental perspective and not vice-versa. These issues include the practical difficulties of bringing up their child, their relationship to various formal services with whom they have contact, and the problems of obtaining information. In each case the analysis is extended by considering occasions when, in the context of professional files or professional-parent encounters, the same issues also arise. It is worth noting that the various difficulties with practicalities, services and information reported by parents in this study are very similar to previous studies, whether the framework is disabled children (Philp and Duckworth, 1982) mentally-handicapped children (Hannam, 1980) or Educationally Sub-Normal (Severe) children (Reid, 1979). The final two chapters represent re-edited versions of proposals that were originally presented to every participant in the research, professionals and parents respectively, during 1984. As such they represent a somewhat naive, and arguably misguided, attempt by the researcher to influence practice. They do, however, contain certain themes that are worth pointing out. Firstly, that parents' difficulties can only be resolved by reclaiming a degree of responsibility over their own lives through collective action. Furthermore, that their problems are best conceptualized as both ordinary and collective problems. Secondly, there is the hope that professionals may come to regard their procedures and their existence as a category of person as problematic. And finally, that significant change for people with mental handicaps and their families depends ultimately on ending inequalities of class, gender and race, as well as of disability.

Indeed, this work does not go on to examine the inequalities and divergence of interests between parents and children. In fact it continues to use the out-dated terms 'mental handicap' and 'educationally sub-normal' which are increasingly being rejected by those so labelled. This is partly because the research pre-dates the implementation of the 1981 Education Act. As such it is an important historical record of the language of professionals in particular, but also parents, at that time. But even the more recent terminology such as 'children with learning difficulties' does not resolve the issue. The new terms continue to individualize problems and isolate people. Such terms draw attention away from 'teachers with teaching difficulties', 'educational systems with social control difficulties', and 'political economies with legitimation difficulties'. The struggle over language is a reflection of a much wider and more complex political struggle.

One final point might be made about values and research. I would argue that there is a methodological advantage in acknowledging rather than trying to exclude my politics. To paraphrase William Foote Whyte's comment on participant observation and apply it to the issue of political commitment in research: I found the answers to questions I would not otherwise have had the sense to ask.

Chapter Two

THE PROCESS OF RESEARCH

In the early stages, the research was very much guided by the practicalities of sources of data I was able to gain access to. The region studied was selected on the basis of having personal contacts (see below for a full discussion) and the lack of such contacts proved decisive in being unable to replicate the study in another area. The study was centred around relatively young mentally-handicapped children because this was a means of looking at more recent developments in their social situation. In practice the focus on children attending special school also meant that the research centred on children living at home. This reflected certain concerns of the research in that, firstly what I felt I had to say amounted to more than criticizing residential services as inappropriate, but secondly I had also written an undergraduate dissertation based on research carried out at the local Educationally Sub-Normal (Moderate) school (Dyson, 1981), a factor which influenced the development of this study. In particular this influenced the decision to look at files kept by the professionals, as I had been appalled to discover, in the earlier research, the extent to which moral and social value-judgements are made by professionals, without any means of redress for the subjects.

The more technical aspects of how the sample was selected and other details of method are included in appendices at the end of the book. The research was centred around a group of twenty children attending a school for Educationally Sub-Normal (Severe) pupils in the East Midlands (see Appendix 1). For simplicity the terms

'ESN(S)' and 'mentally-handicapped' are used inter-
changeably though it is recognized that not all children
who attend ESN(S) schools are necessarily mentally-handicapped. The main fieldwork took place between April
1982 and April 1983. The children (twelve boys, eight
girls) were aged between two and twelve when the
parents (or foster-parents) were interviewed in April-May
1982. The interviews were taped in the parents' homes
and focussed on any difficulties the parents had with
practical problems, services or information. The files held
by professionals on the same twenty children were also
looked at. These included the files kept at the ESN(S)
school; the Schools Psychological Service; the General
Hospital (where the paediatricians were based); the
Community Health Services (where the medical officer
worked) and the assessment unit at a residential hospital
for the subnormal. Only the Social Services refused
permission for me to see the relevant files. Finally,
various meetings between parents and professionals were
taped. These included twelve paediatric clinics at the
General Hospital; four case-conferences held at the
ESN(S) school; two assessments of a child carried out by
the medical officer in the child's home, and two meetings
involving an educational psychologist (see Appendix 2 for
how these various sources of data were distributed). In
addition a fieldwork diary was kept which recorded
informal conversations that took place with parents and
professionals as well as details of other schools, clinics,
training-centres and social work meetings visited.

The technical details of the interviews are dealt
with particularly in Appendices 3 and 4. In addition to
representing the viewpoint of those who have to find
practical ways of living with the mentally-handicapped,
the interviews with the parents fulfilled other theoretical
conditions. Firstly, with such a small sample it was felt
that interviews which as far as possible permitted parents
to express their own views were necessary in order to
show that their views closely follow the opinions
expressed by similar parents in other research. Secondly,
when considering the files and meetings it is important to
be clear that the subjects of such records and encounters
are not atypical in some way (see Appendix 5).

Reviewing the official files was the chosen method
of ascertaining the points of view of the various
professionals (see Appendix 1). It could be argued that

this was necessary because being myself the brother of a mentally-handicapped person means that my own family have connections with the services and under these circumstances the chances of eliciting anything other than professional rhetoric would have been slight. Indeed, under such circumstances an interview with professionals might be said to be logically equivalent to the types of professional-client meetings I later observed. For practical purposes, then, the files were treated as a source of information on the viewpoints of the professionals.

The procedure was to copy certain extracts from the professionals' letters contained in the files. Apart from the various social and moral judgements which I had expected to find, these included comments on the abilities or conditions of the child as well as comments on the attitudes, opinions and behaviour of the parents and/or the child. Those files seen after the parents had been interviewed were also reviewed in terms of criteria influenced by the interviews. Thus extracts were made concerning any comments about the practical problems of parents bringing up their mentally-handicapped children; about their own or other professional services, and about the releasing of information to parents. Furthermore, any information which was apparently self-contradictory or that contradicted other data from interviews or meetings was also noted.

In view of the fieldwork diary that was kept, many informal or incidental conversations with the parents and professionals were subject to relatively systematic recording. In therefore being able to reflect on the research process, to consider how one was treated by the subjects of the research, another possible source of research information is opened up. This information can serve to highlight the main data of the research, but can also tell the researcher something about the methods that were used. To begin with, the notes from the fieldwork diary reinforce the findings from the interviews with regard to the parents' problems with practicalities, services and information.

PRACTICAL PROBLEMS

At the beginning of one interview, before the recorder was switched on, one mother explained that she had got up from her sickbed to do the interview. She had been laid up with a bad back from the strain of lifting her eight-year-old child who could not walk. The precarious nature of some of the children's lives was forcibly brought home to me by the occasions when, in trying to arrange interviews or meetings, the parents apologized that this would not be possible straight away since the child had been very ill and taken into hospital or had even, in one case, had to undergo yet another major life-saving operation. The problems that parents have with transport to the hospital were illustrated by the three occasions I was able to give the mother and child a lift to the hospital by way of small recompense for permission to tape the paediatric clinics. The social isolation that mothers of handicapped children (and, of course, mothers of young children) can suffer was suggested by the number of times, when calling at the house in connection with obtaining permission, arranging meetings or distributing the final report, the mothers were very keen to talk, saying they were pleased to see me because they were often stuck in the house all day with no-one to talk to.

DIFFICULTIES WITH SERVICES

The parents' difficulties in dealing with the services were often illustrated by their attitudes and comments to me as a researcher. In attending the paediatric clinics with the parents I made it a policy to meet the parents and child at outpatients (unless they were being given a lift in which case they were picked up from home) and experience what turned out to be the frustrations of waiting with them. Two parents stressed that I would have to be on time if not early as they claimed that if they were late they had to wait ages. One mother whose waiting-time extended to nearly two hours expressed the hope that a neighbour would take in her other young child who was due home from school for lunch. Another mother, though called on time when I accompanied her, also mentioned that a regular problem was getting neighbours to look out for other children due home from school for lunch, in case she was late back from the clinic. In general the waiting-area for the clinics was crowded and noisy, though well-stocked with toys, and there was a charity worker to play with the children. The basic problem remained, however, of keeping the handicapped child and its siblings amused for relatively long periods of time. On one occasion I was left literally 'holding the baby' as the only possible way the mother could get a drink for herself and the children. Indeed the number of times I could help by holding or entertaining children, carrying prescription slips, carrying bags etc., gave some indication of the difficulties parents might usually face. When fathers attended the clinics, they tended to become impatient more quickly than the mothers through the frustrations, one father observing that if it was a business it would have to be closed down. On one occasion during an actual clinic I felt very guilty about contributing to the overwhelming numbers of professionals facing the parents and child in the clinic. In addition to the paediatrician, the parents, and the child there were two nurses (one coming and going), two junior doctors, two medical students and myself.

Often the insensitivities of the doctors and nurses at the clinics showed themselves. If they talked to the parents at all it was often only through me. Doctors and nurses apologized to me during the course of long periods of waiting, not to the parents. One consultant even explained to me the reasons why a child would be seeing a junior doctor that day, without addressing the remarks also to the parents. Of course my presence changed the situation, but even in the changed situation the greater concern shown me represented an insult to the parents and child. Several parents commented either before or after the clinic that they often went through the 'same old routine' to little effect. Indeed, one mother pointed out that the paediatrician was simply not aware of the difficulties caused by referring the child back to the GP because of the various appointments, waiting and general routines that would have to be gone through for the child to see the GP. Moreover, one example indicates how professionals may tend to view situations more in terms of the difficulties that may be created for themselves. I accompanied a clinical medical officer to one family's home to observe this doctor testing the developmental progress of the child. Talking to the head-teacher of the special school about it the next day, the head-teacher commented that she had heard that the child had not been very co-operative.

Surprising though it may seem, a constant theme from informal conversations with various professionals responsible in some way for the children was how the mentally-handicapped were not central to their work, even in some cases that they were marginal to the central concerns of the professionals job. The senior clinical medical officer pointed out that his jurisdiction included a variety of special schools. He also noted that his work had become more of a matter of dealing with administrative concerns. The educational psychologists claimed that seventy per cent of their work was with children from mainstream schools, and that of these over ninety per cent would be remaining in ordinary classes. The social workers were in a 'team' for the mentally-handicapped which also doubled as the geriatric team. In compiling an advisory booklet on local services for the handicapped one social worker said she had been embarrassed to discover herself what few facilities there were for the mentally-handi-capped. Even the staff of the assessment centre based at a hospital emphasized that the centre was for children in general not just handicapped children.

There were several indicators which suggested that it would be correct to interpret some of the main findings as the professionals imposing their stereotypes on the parents and children. For example, whilst travelling with the clinical medical officer to a house-visit, he stopped the car and got out to speak to two young partially-sighted people who had in the past attended a special school under his jurisdiction. On returning to the car the medical officer expressed his doubts about the couple's plans to get married because they 'don't appreciate how handicapped they are'. Humanitarian concern, it seems, can be linked to professional stereotyping. Or again, both the clinical medical officer and a paediatrician contrast two children (a different two in each case) describing one as exemplifying the optimistic side of their work (because the child had improved with regard to the doctors' tests) and the other as typifying the pessimistic cases they had to deal with (because they felt the child would not show any improvement when tested again in a few months' time). In general the interpretation of professional stereotyping is further confirmed by the manner in which the name of a 'problem case' can bring a smile to the faces of professionals gathered for a case-conference. This process of stereotyping would seem to be encouraged by the manner in which professionals refer to '<u>mother</u> says ...' or '<u>mum</u>'s a bit anxious' rather than refer to 'Mrs. X'.

<u>Related</u> to this question of stereotyping, it also soon became clear during the course of the research that the professionals had very clear ideas of what factors a sociologist ought to be studying in connection with the mentally-handicapped. The senior clinical medical officer thought that the information I should look for in the files was to see how such factors as parental age, number of siblings, position of child in family affected the ways the parents brought up the child. The consultant from the assessment hospital thought I should try and identify which factors would enable professionals to persuade parents to keep their children at home and not seek long-term residential care. These impressions serve to reinforce some of the main findings that professionals have definite ideas about how the children <u>should</u> be brought up and thereby what, in their view, constitutes 'good' and 'bad' parenting.

Some of the services - in particular the assessment hospital where there was provision for long-stay residential care - provided clues as to what it might be like for the parents to relate to them by their defensive attitude, anticipating criticism they thought that the research might make of them. One consultant at the assessment hospital was scathing about a previous researcher who had been given board and lodgings while the research was done, and who had then written a highly critical report advancing his/her career, without even having had the courtesy to give the hospital a copy of the report. When the conversation was repeated several months into the research, I volunteered the information that my report was likely to be critical too. The consultant promised to take me to court if I wrote anything that was not true, and suggested several distinctions between what would and would not be appropriate. 'Appropriate' seemed to include letting the hospital have a copy of the report (which I eventually did) and being constructive in criticisms. Sociologists, the consultant argued, should be "in the business of" proposing and establishing alternatives so that the long-stay hospitals would no longer be necessary. The consultant also anticipated criticism that parents were not able to see files written about them and their children. The almost incredible justification offered for this (namely that closed professional files balanced the opportunity that parents had to write letters to their relations, letters that professionals would never see, criticizing those professionals!) suggests that some professionals have no conception of the power that devolves to them through the opportunity to construct secret official records. Indeed the language some professionals from the assessment unit used to describe their relationship to the parents suggests that some professionals themselves believe in the illusion that the professional-client relationship can be an equal partnership. The language is permeated with capitalist jargon. The assessment unit (and other professionals) were "in the business of" trying to make "contracts" with the parents and "sell" reluctant parents "deals". The capitalist makes contracts with the worker, but of course this is neither equal nor fair.

When allowing me access to certain information certain professionals apologized that I might not find much data - or at least not much data of interest to my research. In retrospect, this seems to confirm certain grievances that the parents have with regard to the services. Two paediatricians each wondered whether I would get anything out of attending the clinics, a first hint to the later findings that the paediatricians regarded the clinics as very much routine, and that the parents wondered what they were getting out of attending the clinics. Similarly, a psychologist warned that I would not find very much written in the files about some of the children, which seems to correspond to the parents' uncertainties about if and how their child had been seen by a psychologist, but also gives the impression that Schrag and Divoky (1981) are correct to argue that complete files are indications of the competence of professionals. Presumably, in an area such as mental handicap where there is uncertainty about what can be done, professionals worry about being comprehensive, and (hence the remarks to me) being seen to be comprehensive. One psychologist from the study and another at a conference I attended remarked that ESN(M) provision was the contentious area of special education, suggesting therefore that special schools for the severely mentally-handicapped are not contentious, that they are the natural, logical, obvious place for such children to be sent, which corresponds to the way parents were apparently first introduced to the idea of special schooling.

PROBLEMS WITH INFORMATION

Perhaps the most revealing incident of the research process arose from the worst methodological and moral error of the study, namely that I reviewed most of the children's files without explicit written permission from the parents. I visited all the parents; explained what I had done; offered my apologies; asked if despite this grave ethical mistake I could still use the data, and if they would be prepared to sign a permission form retrospectively. To my surprise all twenty families agreed to this arrangement, but equally interesting were their reactions generally. Some thought that they had effectively given me permission through having made general offers to help my research all they could after I had interviewed them. Others thought that it did not matter because they would have given me permission if I had asked, or because they would not have known that I had seen the files if I had not called to apologize. Two parents did not even know that such files were kept on their children. Several others said that they would go along with whatever the professionals thought was best (which suggests at least that I was viewed as something akin to a representative of the professionals by some parents). One mother said this did not matter because she did not approve of professional records, quoting an instance from a clinic where a junior doctor pretended to find a minor physical deformity in the child because it was in the notes, though subsequent to the notes being written the deformity had been found not to exist after all. Several other parents laughingly joked that I was forgiven and wondered whether I had got into trouble over the matter either with my university tutor or with any of the doctors or other professionals. These parents, it might be suggested, viewed me as distinct from the professionals. Indeed this type of response was associated with those parents who knew of my personal experience with regard to mental handicap. Finally there were two parents who seemed (and very reasonably so) annoyed but who regarded the apology as sufficient to redeem the situation. But why did such an insulting mistake not lead to greater anger, mass withdrawal from the research, even legal action? One possibility is that the general experience of bringing up a mentally-handicapped child has left these parents with a rather fatalistic outlook concerning their relative powerlessness. Another is that some of the parents were not aware of how the existence of files written about them and their children might affect them (e.g. that decisions could be made on the basis of 'information' they cannot check or challenge). Indeed the professionals seem to have been successful in imposing their definition on the files as "theirs", a definition that was even reflected in my phraseology, referring to 'doctors' files' and so on. Then again, the parents may have disapproved more of the keeping of files than of my failure to seek permission to see them. But perhaps the overriding reason for the parents' reactions was a general deference with regard to people in authority, or presumed to be in authority. So much so that it seemed the parents had been somehow taught to devalue their own viewpoints and their own rights. But whatever the reason the error in failing to keep parents informed adds a sharpness to the parents' argument that they do not receive good quality information, or even any information at all in some cases, from the professionals. It is interesting to note that with the exception of the consultant from the assessment hospital none of the other professionals asked me to obtain written permission from the parents before I had access to the respective files, the doctors feeling this arrangement to be acceptable because I had interviewed the parents, even though I explicitly pointed out that I had not sought written agreement from the parents. From the sum of informal conversations associated with obtaining access to the files various professionals suggested a range of justifications for not allowing parents to read the files, and these are discussed later.

Several other instances from the research process give pointers to the problems that parents have in securing accurate information from the professionals. In one instance an educational psychologist told me that he had not informed a mother about the probability that she would lose her entitlement to the attendance allowance when the child moved school because he did not think it was his place to do so. This seemed a very weak excuse until I considered my position as a researcher and realized I had also failed to inform the mother of this important information. On another occasion after I had watched a psychologist assess a child at school I met the mother in the general course of the research, and bringing up this assessment in conversation found that this was the first she knew of it. Again this was a moral failure on my part to obtain permission from the parents, but it also indicated two aspects to the problems of information that the parents had. Firstly that they are not kept informed by professionals about what is happening, but also, secondly, that professionals (including sociologists) tend to behave as if the place of a child in a special school is reason enough not to have to seek permission to approach the child, as if parents and child thereby forfeit their rights to be consulted. The problems concerning information have many aspects. The professionals themselves may not have the knowledge, as with the social workers who during the series of meetings with the parents often turned to me because they did not know the answers to parents' questions about the services. Or there may be no established method of giving the parents even relatively straightforward information. For example, when distributing copies of the report to the subjects of the study, I found that both the relevant social workers had moved on from their posts. Later the same day whilst taking a copy to one of the families I was able to inform the mother that the 'welfare worker' she was expecting had in fact changed jobs. Sometimes information does not reach the parents in a clear form. One set of parents who professed to be totally confused about precisely what the paediatrician had been trying to tell them asked my advice about whether they should ask the reception nurse to go back to the doctor to try and establish what had been said. On other occasions it is not the process of communication but the nature of the information itself which is confusing. Once when sitting in the staff-room the special-school teachers were discussing the non-informative character of some medical and psychological explanations, complaining in particular about their circularity (e.g. the child has this syndrome because he/she behaves that way, and behaves this way because he/she has that syndrome). This brings us to a consideration of what the research process reveals about relations between professionals.

RELATIONS BETWEEN PROFESSIONALS

Informal conversations with two psychologists told me much about their view of the changing roles of special education and of special teachers. After an assessment in which the psychologist consistently stressed what the child concerned could not do, the psychologist implied that the teacher was too emotionally involved, describing her as "gushing". The psychologist ventured that the teacher was insecure because she was more in the fashion of the old-style caring minder in special education than the newer professionally-trained teachers. This related as well to more general criticisms of an ESN(S) school on an old site which had recently moved to new purpose-built accommodation and simultaneously acquired a younger professionally-trained head-teacher. The psychologists also said they felt they ought to "come clean" about their attitude to the assessment hospital. They claimed that this was not a question of professional antagonism, particularly since they acknowledged that the system of phased care operating there had proved its worth. But they questioned the necessity for a child to undergo yet another assessment (usually over a period of 2-3 weeks) that took the child out of its natural setting and produced no radically new suggestions for the child's management. They suggested that these assessments and the subsequent reassessments were part of the hospital's struggle to maintain its clientele. They also saw the medical officer as the smoothing link at case-conferences between the medically-dominated environment of the hospital and the community-based services.

On the other hand the consultant at the assessment hospital complained that educational psychologists made very poor contributions to the case-conference held at the end of assessments, and that the social workers were in general even worse, though on rare occasions they could make the best contributions. The social workers complained that they were dependent on the paediatricians and the medical officer to refer clients to them, which they often would not do for reasons of claimed confidentiality. Meanwhile, the senior clinical medical officer complained that one paediatrician did not always take enough responsibility for making decisions. The medical officer also expressed some reservations about the value of the assessments at the hospital, and also about the value of physiotherapy for children with multiple handicaps who 'would never learn to walk anyway'. He also referred to some antagonism between the special school teachers and the teacher attached to the assessment unit because the latter would write reports on the child for the case conference on the basis of two weeks' experience which contradicted the views of the school teachers who would have known the child much longer. Finally, the head-teacher pointed out that she was caught in the middle between the medical officer's assessment of a child and what the parents claimed they knew their child was capable of.

These various professional rivalries suggest another possible source of problems for the parents with regard to the services and information which may emerge if professionals try to maintain a united front to the parents rather than try to explain professional differences of opinion. This leads us to consider how professionals apparently feel that they should judge the appropriateness of parents, not vice-versa.

JUDGING THE 'APPROPRIATENESS' OF PARENTS

The idea that professionals judge how appropriately they feel the parents are bringing up their mentally-handicapped child was first suggested by the reactions of some parents to being interviewed. One father apparently viewed the questions as designed to test the parents' memory, frequently asking his wife if they were sure they were answering correctly. Several parents seemed embarrassed when talking about having received 'charity' from such organizations as the Rowntree Trust. As a researcher I was frequently shown into what I took to be the family's best room and was often shown a great deal of deference. This sometimes took the form of addressing me as 'doctor', and one mother, having misunderstood the original letter, phoned me up and asked where she had to bring her child to see me. The degree of deference shown seemed to increase in relation to lower socio-economic status and to minimal criticism of the services. This strongly suggested to me that such defensive reactions indicated a sensitiveness to the possibility of being judged 'bad' parents by various professionals or authorities. Three parents felt they had to apologize for criticizing the services, and one mother was extremely careful not to reveal the names of the doctors she was talking about. With hindsight, the actions of some parents at interview might be interpreted as showing off the abilities of their child (reciting nursery rhymes, performing feats of memory, imitating TV characters) as evidence that they themselves are 'good' parents. They are likely to be 'rewarded' by comments such as the nurse who told one mother and father that they were "the best parents in the world".

Conversely there seemed to be evidence from some of the informal contact with professionals that the latter were indeed involved in evaluating the parents. The staff from the assessment unit criticized two parents from the sample by name for not having made use of the services in the 'correct' manner. The assessment staff, teachers, and educational psychologists all criticized a variety of parents for the way they disciplined (or not) the mentally-handicapped child. Parents who were known to have voiced criticisms of the services were then criticized for having the audacity to continue to use the services! In one instance the professionals agreed to use the "carrot" of the opportunity for a child to learn a new language technique in order to force the parents to work on behaviour control of the child. Similarly after the medical officer assessed a child with the parents pointing out the child's performance was depressed by being ill, the medical officer asked me if the child had behaved in a similar way when I had attended a clinic with the parents and child a few days previously. This I took as an attempt to test the judgement of the parents. It is in the light of these indications that I then looked at how parents sometimes use professional jargon about themselves and their child, namely, because professional approval is won by doing so. For example, one mother described herself as a "typical 'reluctant mother'", which I also felt related to her past status as a professional, having previously been a nurse. The idea of winning professional approval because of sensing being evaluated might also be argued to be feeding in to the acceptance of a change in the definition of the situation, if this is instigated by a professional. Thus a mother said her child 'must be better than we thought' because the educational psychologist was arranging to transfer the child to the ESN(M) school.

Finally, and perhaps most importantly, what can the

process of research tell us about the particular research methods employed?

RESEARCH PROCESS AND RESEARCH METHODS

1. The Files

With hindsight perhaps the most decisive factors in obtaining access to the various medical, educational and psychological files were the indirect personal links I had with the services. As the brother of a mentally-handicapped person, with my family living in the area studied, one paediatrician and the medical officer already knew me by name and therefore had some reference point from which to gauge my request. Having also studied the local ESN(M) school as part of an undergraduate course, this also gave the head-teacher of the ESN(S) school and the psychologists a referent. At an early stage of the research an attempt was made to set up in another area a replication of the research eventually completed. Thinking back, it was probably the lack of personal referents, and the consequent need to be that much more erudite in explaining the aims and means of research, that led to my failure to persuade the teachers and psychologists in the other area whom I approached to allow me access to files as part of any research. And it was probably the sense of personal failure and embarrassment experienced through these refusals, as much as lack of time, that dissuaded me from pursuing the idea of replication. Indeed the personal links I had in the area eventually studied may help to explain why the paediatricians and the clinical medical officer did not ask me to see an ethics committee, but thought it sufficient to introduce me to their respective administrative superiors. Being allowed to see hospital files containing paediatricians' letters was important in breaking through a vicious circle of initial refusals of permission to see various files because they contained letters from a variety of professionals, not just those of the particular professional I was asking. These various considerations help to explain (but not excuse) the way in which I became so tied up with my own view of the problems of access to files that the moral and legal rights of the parents to be consulted became secondary.

The other main methodological issue concerning the files in relationship to the rest of the research is the significance of the particular twenty sets of parents chosen. To judge from the father's occupation as recorded on file they covered a wide range of socio-economic statuses (see Appendix 5). Furthermore, apart from the fact that the children all attended the same ESN(S) school, they were not a group who could be easily fitted into other categories used by professionals. The clinical medical officer, for example, expressed the view that he could not understand how I had chosen my sample as the children did not all have the same aetiology or syndrome; they were not all the same age; they were not all 'special care' (i.e. multiply-handicapped) children; they did not even live in the main town of the area - thirteen lived in smaller towns or villages nearby. However, from the point of view of the issues raised by the research, whether the twenty are in any way representative in terms of class or urban-rural location matters less than the important factor they have in common. They are all parents (or foster parents) whose handicapped child lives at home with them. That is, they have not had their child adopted or placed in long-term residential care, and the latter claims Wilkin (1979) is in any case not related to social class but to factors such as increasing age of the child; greater problems with the child's physical health; the degree of functional incapacity of the child; the degree of supervision required; the degree of social maturity and the extent of behaviour problems. Therefore, the main drawback to the representativeness of the twenty parents is not the numbers in each social class, nor even the positivistic concern that they are all from one area, but that the viewpoints of parents whose handicapped child no longer lives at home with them, are excluded. And bearing in mind the findings of Wilkin (1979) it seems reasonable to assume that the problems identified in this research are an under-estimation of the difficulties facing parents of mentally-handicapped children generally.

2.   The Parental Interviews

In fifteen out of the twenty cases both the mother and father were present at the taped interview, with the mothers usually providing the majority of the explanations, presumably reflecting their greater role in the day-to-day care of the child. In four cases the mother only was interviewed, and in one case the mother and grandmother were interviewed. The differences (if any) between the perspectives of the mother and father were not the main focus of research, though as we shall see several of the professionals were prepared to offer pseudo-psychological accounts of the dynamics of family life.

In the early interviews I felt particularly awkward and unskilled at drawing out comments from the parents, factors not helped by the lack of a pilot study. It was often the amusement surrounding mistakes that relieved any tension (e.g. forgetting to switch on the recorder, having to borrow a recorder, having the child continually attempt to turn the recorder off etc.). Some of the parents, too, were evidently worried about the interview. A few took up the offer in the original letter (Appendix 3) to confirm who I was with the head-teacher of the school. Others talked to parents who had been interviewed before it came to their turn. And in many cases the interview would be concluded, the tape-recorder switched off, only for conversation to start up again if I was offered a cup of tea, and some of the most interesting points went unrecorded as the parents relaxed after the 'official' interview was over. This 'lost' conversation was then written up from memory in the fieldwork diary.

Another factor affecting what was said during the interviews was if the parents asked me before, after or at all why I was interested in mental handicap, which I explained as being a personal interest because of my brother. This meant that some parents went through the interview knowing I had a personal interest in mental handicap, whereas others did not. Those who did not may have viewed me more as someone 'checking' to see if they were responding 'appropriately' to the services, which may in turn have led them to underestimate the problems and criticisms they had. On the other hand, those who knew of the personal reasons behind my interest were more prepared to expound criticisms but conversely also tended to stop short of explaining some problems or criticisms because they felt they could appeal to a commonsense knowledge we both shared by saying "you know".

3.   The Clinics and Meetings
One of the key factors here is obviously the extent to which the interaction is changed by the presence of a researcher. At one stage the head-teacher of the ESN(S)

school informed me that parents who were attending clinics at which I was present were pointing out to her later that my presence led to a shortening of the waiting time and to being paid more attention in the clinic itself. In making conversation with one mother I made the bad mistake of pointing this out, because she was then disappointed that she had to wait just as long as usual as the 'researcher effect' did not operate in the same way in that instance. After the clinics several of the parents commented that they experienced clinics as taking up their time without having anything to show for it.

One or two instances concerning various other occasions when the parents met professionals served to remind me of certain similarities between my position and that of the professionals. With only twenty names to remember I still often had to think quickly and hard to remember the child's name - an indication that professionals deal with many handicapped children relatively superficially and briefly, whereas the parents deal with their one (usually) handicapped child but in depth. The difference has affinities with the methodological debate about the balance between reliability and validity. I was also somewhat shocked to discover that I was developing some of the same strategies as professionals quite independently of them. For example, when accompanying the medical officer to assess the child at home, the medical officer parked his car a short distance away from the house explaining it saved the embarrassment of searching for the correct house. A few months earlier when interviewing the parents I had parked my car in the same place for the same reason.

4. The Report for the Parents and Professionals

By the time an 18,000 word report was written, typed, printed and distributed in person to the parents and professionals nearly two and a half years had elapsed since the first interview. Not surprisingly some of the parents had to stop and think to remember who I was. Several said that they were pleased to receive some feedback, and three parents said that because of the length of time they had waited they had begun to think that my offer to give them a report was to be just another unfulfilled promise by a professional. One mother asked for my opinion - my honest opinion - about whether my report would have any effect on the services. I admitted that I seriously doubted whether there would be any change for the better as a result of my report, but added that it was important to continue to argue one's beliefs, if only because it would be more absurd to allow the present situation to continue by default. A further two years had elapsed before I was able to send each parent and professional an offprint of an article written on the basis of the research (Dyson, 1986).

USE OF ABBREVIATIONS/SYMBOLS

In the empirical chapters which now follow various abbreviations have been used to report taped conversation as indicated below:-

AU	Assessment Unit
DR	Doctor (including paediatricians, consultants, registrars, medical officers - used generically when need to maintain confidentiality)
EP	Educational Psychologist
F	Father (sometimes referred to as Mr. X)
GM	Grandmother
HT	Head-teacher of ESN(S) School
HV	Health visitor
M	Mother (sometimes referred to as Mrs. X)
MO	Senior Clinical Medical Officer
SMD	Simon Dyson
ST	Speech Therapist
SW	Social Worker
T	Teacher at ESN(S) School
X	The mentally-handicapped child

.....	pause in conversation (proportional to length of pause)
(.....)	section of one person's speech omitted (if on a separate line this means a whole section of conversation omitted)
/	sudden break in conversation (representing an interruption or a sudden change in direction by same speaker)
(person)	person or place identified in abstract for reasons of confidentiality
(laughs)	description of behaviour
(i.e. -)	explanatory note
(((	spoken simultaneously
----->	speaker talks through interruption

Chapter Three

PRACTICAL DIFFICULTIES

PRACTICAL PROBLEMS: INTERVIEWS WITH THE
PARENTS

The various practical problems which emerged from the
interviews may be thought of in four broad categories.
The problems of the child's ability to be mobile and to
communicate may be thought of as problems because the
period of childhood is being prolonged. Sleeping, feeding,
and toileting problems represent difficulties which prolong
the work a mother does in caring for a child. Difficulties
with transport, employment, holidays and health reflect
some of the general disadvantages of the place of women
in society. Problems with hospital, housing and special
equipment are problems which many families have but
which the families of mentally-handicapped children suffer
more frequently.

(a) Mobility
Nearly half of the sample of twenty children were not
mobile in ways that meant they nearly always had to be
carried.

> F   "As he's getting bigger and older he's
> getting more difficult. From that point of
> view.
>
> M   Obviously you can't just go wherever you
> wish to go and hope that he'll go along
> and be OK. You've got to consider him all
> the time.

> F Oh everything centres round him. He has to be carried everywhere. He/you know, he can walk, but he walks where he wants to go. Then if he chooses not to walk he'll just sit down and there's no way you can make him walk. So you've got to carry him."

But in some ways this under-estimates the problem as the combination of non-mobility and severe mental handicap may be the difference between the child living at home or in hospital, as Wilkin (1979) has shown.

Furthermore, children who are considered mentally-handicapped may take a lot longer than usual in learning to walk, as was the case with a quarter of this group. Two parents had no problems with their child walking at first but then had problems as their child became too strong and active to manage easily.

(b) Communication

More than two-thirds of the children had problems with communication - being completely unable to talk, or else not being able to make themselves understood either to parents or to strangers.

> M "I think the main problem at the moment is that she doesn't talk very much so .... communication is quite difficult for her. We can understand most of what she wants but sort of to strangers .... it/she has trouble."

(c) Sleeping

Over half of the parents reported having disturbed nights over long periods.

> M "He's a terrible sleeper. He never sleeps hardly at all. He's crying half the night most nights. But as yet we put up with it. You know (..) It's usually a dozen times a night now I get out to him. Turn him over. He can't turn or anything like that you see either."

(d) Feeding

Over half the parents reported a variety of problems associated with feeding the child. These included slow feeding, under-feeding, over-feeding, regurgitating food and allergies to certain types of foods.

> F   "The practical difficulties is trying to feed X, and his sleep. And that's where you really need the help if anything (...) Virtually our life is in the kitchen."

(e) Toileting

More children were still incontinent either during the day or at night, though eleven had some form of help with the provision of free nappy rolls by the Community Health Services.

> M   "'Cause I mean sheets, I mean I've got my washing now. I've got about six sheets in there, I'll guarantee I put a clean sheet on each day. I mean you need two sheets each day with that bleep (i.e. enuresis alarm) how you make it up. It's a lot of washing."

(f) Transport

Although three-quarters of this group had some access to a car, most of these still said that they had had problems with transport. Problems included the physical incapacity of the child, behaviour problems, the cost of transport to hospital, the time that travel took out of the mother's busy working day and the embarrassed reaction of other travellers on public transport.

> GM   "We have to pay for taxis and that sort of thing.
> M   That's right. At one time we were going on the bus weren't we? But in the end it was just too difficult to get on the bus."

Amongst this group school transport was generally considered adequate though one mother had had to fight to get her child a reliable safety harness, and another complained that in snowy weather her child could not go to school as she could not push the wheelchair up the steep hill to the pick-up point.

(g) Employment

In this study one quarter of the fathers had been affected in their jobs by having to take time off work for hospital appointments etc.

> SMD "Do you normally go up to the hospital as well, Mr. X?
>
> F With X? Yes, I normally take her in. It means I probably/well I lose time out of work. If she's an appointment for nine or ten. Well I've got to/I work with two shifts - usually early mornings and late afternoons. If I'm early morning it means I've got to come out of my work about half-past eight to get here in time to take her up the hospital. (...)"

In addition it seems reasonable to suppose that the jobs of another two fathers were affected in that the family consciously moved to this county with the child's welfare in mind. One mother mentioned the problem of combining paid employment with looking after the child and two mothers said that having a handicapped child has disrupted their voluntary or fostering work.

(h) Parents' Health

In the interviews no questions about the health of the parents were asked but two mothers suffered from back problems (indeed one mother got up from her sick-bed to do the interview) and four mentioned having suffered various forms of 'nerves' or depression.

> M "Just lately everything seemed to get on top of me. I mean I'm all right now ... been able to cope. But about a month ago I was really down, my doctor put me on tablets for my nerves. And I just couldn't cope. I couldn't cope because my husband is just getting over hepatitis - that's how he lost his job - which is a long slow illness. And with X and my husband I just

> couldn't cope at all (...) Everything was
> kind of getting on top of me."

This episode is of special importance as it illustrates how an illness arises from practical problems which are social and therefore political issues (the lack of provision to help with the practical problems of looking after a mentally-handicapped child; the expectation that the mother should cope with enormous burdens of work without pay or recognition; the 'free enterprise' system which means employers are free to ignore the contingencies of long illness in a worker). The illness is then defined as a medical problem and treated with drugs. A political problem is reduced to a technical medical one.

(i) Holidays

Three parents in this group specifically mentioned a restriction of leisure activities in general, especially in association with the long school holidays in the summer. Two parents in this sample suggested that at one time or another they had not been able to have a holiday because of their child. In addition another six parents had had their holidays restricted in various ways because of the difficulties of looking after their child.

> M   "But little things like you think what will I do when we want to go on holiday in a few years' time and this sort of thing. At the moment we take him. But really even holidays aren't a great success are they? (...)
>
> F   You know, you take him out of his normal routine and he's .... it's just not a holiday is it?"

(j) Hospital

Other studies have suggested a number of ways in which having to spend time in hospital creates problems for parents and child. In this group of 20 children, 6 had been kept in hospital for a period after their birth, 11 had spent time in hospital for assessment and 16 had spent some time in hospital other than for assessment. Eight parents illustrated the point made by Stacey et al (1970) that hospitalization can be a disturbing experience for both the mother and child.

> M   "So we stayed till we'd got her off to
> sleep, and then we left. And we asked one
> of the nurses in the morning if she'd slept
> all right, because we <u>knew</u> that she
> wouldn't because she doesn't at home. And
> she says, well, she says, you were gone
> about ten minutes and she was wide
> awake. And we could see by her face in
> the morning that she'd been crying all
> night (...............) (The doctor) said himself
> it's part of the healing of a child if
> they're, you know, kept calm. They heal
> far quicker than if they're just crying and
> being miserable (...) That was our one -
> hopefully it's not again - episode in
> hospital."

Some of the parents suggested that long periods of time in
hospital had held their child's development back, and a
few mentioned that the need to travel to the hospital
frequently made transport problems that much more
difficult to bear. Even transport provided by the Area
Health Authority did not necessarily solve the problem as
it was not reliable.

(k) Housing

Two parents mentioned that they had made structural
alterations to the house with the child in mind. In one
case this involved building an extension to the house, and
in another case knocking through two rooms to make a
larger one. In addition three parents had taken specific
account of the child's needs when moving house (a
bungalow to avoid stairs or a larger house for more
space).

(l) Special Equipment

The majority of families had received or supplied
themselves with various items of special equipment and
most had encountered problems with it.

> F   "They put a sound of 80 decibels into him

	and he still didn't respond to that with 80 decibels. And apparently the hearing aids that we'd been persevering with for two years couldn't/weren't
M	Sophisticated enough
F	To get it up to that anyway. So here we are thinking that we're getting somewhere and over a two year period persevering with putting these hearing aids back in when he pulls them out and this and that, when they're not powerful enough anyway. I mean absolutely ridiculous."

In fact the most useful pieces of equipment tended to be the most straightforward ones, such as double-buggies or non-slip feeding dishes.

It is important to recognize all these practical difficulties for what they are. They are not distinct problems that suddenly appear when a family has a handicapped child. Rather they are the 'normal' problems of parents bringing up their children, only extended over a longer period of time, and more frequently complicated by there being a number of problems occurring together. For example, mobility and communication are problems partly because the 'normal' stage of the parents' joy at a child's first words or steps arrives late, in a fragile form and often never at all. In the cycle of family life, the work the mother of a so-called 'normal' child does in teaching it to walk and talk eventually lessens the future work for the mother because she no longer has to carry the child or struggle to understand even the simplest of communications. Furthermore, the initial teaching of walking and talking extends over a relatively short period of time, pre-school and often in direct anticipation of the child going to school. For the mother of a handicapped child the circle of doing the work of teaching in order to lessen the work of management is that much harder to break and extends over many years or forever. Similarly, the work the mother does in getting the child to sleep, eat and toilet at the appropriate times and in the appropriate places. Primary schools, apparently, assume that this work has been successfully completed by the mother well before the child goes to school. Also, a mother with young children may quite commonly experience difficulties in using public transport, going on certain types of holiday, having a paid job (because of lack of creche or nursery provision), or may suffer depression and ill-health. Because in the cases of most children these problems occur in the early years of bringing the child up, they may not be recognized as problems as such, even by the mothers themselves. But they are often life-long problems for the mother, and to a lesser extent the father, of a handicapped child. Finally, problems that for a child's family may usually be relatively infrequent (such as the child going into hospital; needing special equipment; or the family needing to move house) are much more common problems for the family of a child with a disability.

FILES AND MEETINGS

This section looks at how and when the practical problems of the parents are dealt with by the professionals in their files and in various meetings.

(a) Professional Knowledge

To professionals the practical difficulties that the parents face may seem trivial (as in Cartwright, 1967, pp. 40-41), or appear as inappropriate for them to deal with when they have the heavy responsibility of establishing categories.

> "There is a minor problem about inco. pads for incontinence." - Files: Assessment Unit.

The professionals may feel that ordinary everyday problems are not part of their technical professional sphere (the historical foundations of professional knowledge are arguably based on ignoring, or even ignorance of, ordinary practical problems). But parents, knowing that professionals have several years' training in their technical knowledge, may themselves come to hold similar views about what is, and what is not, an appropriate problem for a professional to have to deal with:

> SMD "Are there any other sort of practical day-to-day problems?

> M   .... (laughs) He won't keep still.
> F   Sleeping sometimes.
> M   Yes, sleeping sometimes .... Silly
>   noises, horrible noises. Nothing really that
>   ..../you've got to try and master yourselves
>   really haven't we?" - Interview

It therefore seems probable that many of the parents simply do not tell professionals about certain practical problems that they face when bringing up their child, so that the professionals may be unaware of some of the problems the parents face. For example, the files make no mention of the problems of feeding, of the parents' and child's sleeping, and of difficulties with special equipment. Then again, not all the possible contact with professionals actually takes place. For example, only just over half had been seen by an educational psychologist, and even if the psychologist had met the child, the parents may not have been seen.

However, even when the professionals know about the existence of certain practical problems they may be uncertain what the parents expect of them (see Cartwright, 1967, pp. 218-219), and frightened to ask because that would go against an image of themselves as knowledgeable and in control. The consequence of this is that the professional may seem to be making the unspoken assumption that the mother ought to be able to cope with the problem. This may, in turn, make the mother more reluctant to put the situation forward strongly as a problem. This seems to be the case in this paediatric clinic where the problem of incontinence is briefly acknowledged before the doctor moves quickly on to what are (for him) other routine questions.

> DR   "What about her waterworks?
> M   They're fine. They're all right.
> DR   In nappies?
> M   Yes." - Paediatric clinic.

But if the parents do not spell out to the professionals the exact nature of what a practical problem means and how it affects their lives, the professionals may do more than seem to assume that the mother should cope and actually assume that the mother can cope:

"X continues to present management problems within the home but it appears that the parents have reached a level of tolerance which they feel they are able to cope with and do not appear at this stage to want to further modify X's behaviour." - Files: Clinical Psychologist.

If the problem is thus pushed back to the mother in the family, she may then have to all but break down and scream to get any help. It is not only the social services who act only in a crisis, as doctors seem fond of pointing out (fieldwork diary).

"Mrs. X seemed to be getting to the end of her tether, so I have arranged for his admission to (hospital) to try and find out some way of helping." - Files: Paediatrician.

But as we have seen being in hospital can itself be a practical difficulty for the child and the parents. Professionals observe and record the various practical difficulties of the parents, but do not solve them. Observing and recording problems without corresponding practical advice or solutions then creates a false impression that such problems are a distinctive characteristic of the mentally-handicapped. And so for example doctors must be aware of a practical problem because as representatives of medical knowledge in general (to develop Stimson and Webb, 1975, p. 51) they are expected to know about such characteristics even though they may not be required or expected to act towards a solution in any way. An unfortunate consequence of this is that genuine caring and concern by the doctor, separated as it is by the very nature of professional knowledge from an attempt at practical solutions, then seems more like patronizing sympathy:

"The parents at home provide good care although I am sure X's constant over-activity must be very wearing particularly for the mother." - Files: Hospital consultant.

However, a more serious and dangerous consequence is when the practical problems arise because of something the professionals themselves have done. The problem then becomes just another characteristic to be recorded, but there appears to be no evaluation of the professional's action.

> "It seems he was quite aggressive at school which was probably the effect of Ritalen." - Files: Paediatrician.

> "He was then admitted to hospital following which he became very remote and ceased to talk." - Files: Medical officer.

Because of the emphasis on observing and recording differences, practical problems are not only seen to be special characteristics of the handicapped but the special characteristics by which the mentally-handicapped are actually defined. Things that the parents and child experience as problems that need to be solved, the professionals see as factors which confirm that the child is retarded, disabled or handicapped. And so the fact that a child may not be able to walk or talk is not, in the view of some professionals, a problem to be resolved, but a confirmation that the label 'handicapped' is correct.

> "Mr. and Mrs. X are very anxious that X should have physiotherapy in order to enable him to walk unaided. Personally I think this is part of the general pattern of his retardation." Files: Medical officer.

What we are faced with is the fact that parents and professionals are interpreting the situation in very different ways. For the professionals a child is slow to learn to walk because it is retarded. For the parents part of the child's general slowness is because of the problems of being slow to walk. But a combination of administrative, legal and practical pressures on the professionals gives their interpretation added weight. For example, so that a child can be admitted to a special school, there is a legal requirement that a statement on special educational needs be kept (Education Act, 1981). Various doctors and psychologists may see the child, and records made of the child's characteristics. From the legal point of view this is to show that at least a doctor, and perhaps a psychologist as well, have seen the child before it is admitted to special school. And from an administrative point of view this is to record characteristics which make the child 'special' and justify placement in a special school. This encourages the types of interpretations that the professionals regard as their specialized knowledge. But as a result this so-called specialized knowledge comes to include certain features which are not necessary or automatic consequences of being mentally handicapped (e.g. it is not a necessary consequence of being mentally-handicapped that the person cannot read or hold down a job). Therefore this specialized knowledge is confusing the cause (public discrimination) and the effect (no jobs) of the problem. This knowledge also includes various moral judgements made by the professionals. One such judgement is that incontinence is one sign of retardation (many highly intelligent physically disabled adults are incontinent). This judgement is reinforced by a practical pressure, namely that primary school teachers do not have the time and resources to deal routinely with wetting and soiling. Incontinence then becomes not a practical problem for the mother, child and school, but another confirmation that the child is retarded.

> "This patient of yours shows evidence of mild developmental retardation. One aspect of this retardation is the fact that he has not yet been toilet-trained." - Files: Medical officer.

The suggestion seems to be - and here is the second part of this particular moral judgement - that the mother has somehow failed in her duties in not having her child toilet-trained in time for primary school.

> "Dr. A recommended that she attended (ESN(S) school) because X was still in nappies day and night at 41/2 years old. Development was also below her chronological age. X also comes from a poor background." Files: Health visitor.

On the other hand because practical problems are seen to be indicative of lack of development, the work a mother may have contributed in helping her child learn to walk is not recognized. This is because from, say, the medical point of view, the modest progress stems directly from whatever general condition the child is thought to have:

> "When compared to the findings reported to you 12 months ago X has made some very slight progress, most noticeably in her ability to take a few steps by herself." - Files: Medical officer.

In these ways the difference in interpretations leads the professionals to normally judge the way in which the parents respond to a certain practical difficulty. For the mother, because her child is having difficulty learning to talk, a means must be found to overcome the lack of communication because it is holding the general development of the child back. The mother apparently chooses a method in which she either actually believes the child can already speak, but not clearly, or else she acts as though she does, in the hope that by acting consistently in response to the noises the child makes, she can teach the child the meaning of language and clearer speech. This may, of course, be an important part of the way children 'normally' learn to speak. From the professional point of view, in such cases the root of the problem is the child's retardation not its communication. This seems to be the view of both medical and psychological professionals, although the psychologist at least notes the opposite view before rejecting it.

> "These (tests) showed some non-verbal activities that were at or above average, but his scores on verbal sub-tests were still at an 'S' level. I doubt that this is any sort of specific language problem (as opposed to being a general cognitive problem)." - Files: Educational psychologist.

> "Delayed speech and language development as part of the global picture." - Files: Medical officer.

The mother's strategy, based on a different point of view, is then frowned upon:

> "Mrs. X frequently imparts meaning to X's vocalization." - Files: Speech therapist.

This difference in interpretation also causes the professionals to misunderstand what might be the best type of support for the parents. The mother (and this was confirmed in the interview with the parents) wants advice for specific problems not routine reviews or clinics where there may be nothing to discuss (because, as we have seen, neither the parents nor the professionals may see it as relevant for the professionals to deal with certain practical problems). However, the professional's viewpoint sees general retardation as the root of the problem, and what the professionals mean by 'problems' are special difficulties arising from special characteristics of the mentally handicapped and not the ordinary problems of children writ large. This viewpoint of the professionals can lead them to be extremely insulting and insensitive in meetings with the parents. In this example a child's problem in walking has held its general development back (as the mother sees it) whereas for the doctor the child's inability to walk has been a sign of backwardness.

> DR   "You know he's not the little cabbage that we ..../
> M   No. But that's/He never was you know.
> DR   No.
> M   I mean I always knew that (laughs). It was bringing it out." - Visit by medical officer.

The differences and characteristics, which are observed by the professionals, become professional knowledge when they are recorded in professional files. In this way the observations take on the appearance of indisputable 'facts'. What is written in the medical records, for example, can be referred to as 'facts' by the doctor if he is trying to persuade the parents about anything (to develop Stimson and Webb, 1975, p.54). This keeping of records is given a further impetus by any requirements made of doctors by the National Health Service over records for hospital administration, by Medical Defence Societies over records for legal protection or by the Local Education Authority over records for referring a child to a special school. Consequently when doctors (and psychologists) are testing children to establish the exact nature of their differences, they are thinking first and foremost about the observations and their future as 'facts' in professional files. The result of this is that the parents' practical problems, such as the child not talking or being too active, are then only mentioned insofar as the difficulty may affect the results of the professionals' tests:

> "Once again the boy proved to be hyperactive and difficult to test. Nevertheless, I think my findings are probably a fair reflection of his ability level." Files: Medical officer.

In other words there is a mismatch between the practical problems as experienced by the parents, and the way professionals react to those problems in various meetings between professionals and parents. For example, the Senior Clinical Medical Officer may ask a mother about her child's talking without necessarily having a practical means of help in mind but mainly to keep his records on the child's developments up to date. In the clinic a paediatrician may ask about a whole range of practical problems - feeding, walking, talking, the parents' health - but not to make suggestions about how the problems may be resolved. The questions are directed towards gathering medical knowledge about the child's level of development physically, socially and intellectually, and as such they are part of the routine of the clinic. Indeed, the paediatrician may become preoccupied with the clinic routine. For example, having talked to a child for several minutes (and having received replies from the child) in order to estimate the child's level of social and intellectual development, the paediatrician then asks the mother about the hearing and speech as if he had not just talked to the child.

> DR   "And his hearing?
> M   His hearing's all right as far as I know, yes.
> DR   And his speech?
> M   His speech is improving (inaudible)
> DR   What/is there still any difficulty ... with clarity?
> M   Er, just a slight bit, that's all." - Paediatric clinic.

It may be that the doctor is considering the possibility of a minor hearing loss. But the doctor may also be deliberately checking up on the mother to see if the information she gives the doctor is balanced and trustworthy (see Davis, 1982, pp. 113-115). If this is the case, then obviously the paediatrician has become so taken up with the clinic routine and accurate records that he is insulting and morally judging the mother as well as not recognizing the practicalities of the problem for the mother. Indeed, the clinic routine can take over so much that the nature of the practical problem, or even whether there is a problem at all, can be completely passed by. For example, the paediatrician does not seem to notice how one mother and father are disagreeing with each other about the extent of a practical problem as they answer a series of routine questions about the child's communication. The father's explanations of the child's progress with regard to communication sound slightly 'pessimistic'. According to him the child has regressed; does not make a double-sound; drones; whines; does not babble, and does not respond to sentences. The mother's explanations sound more 'optimistic'. The child sings; responds; seems to talk at night, and does talk. On other occasions the mother and father agree more closely. The paediatrician fails to comment on this which may suggest that he is concerned with the standard of communication reached by the child and not with how the mother or father experience the practical difficulty of communicating with the child. What suggests that it is the routine clinic questioning, inspired by the keeping of records, which leads to doctors not dealing with practical problems is that when the routine is not their own (as in a school case-conference) they do notice when a problem is not dealt with:

HT   "OK, OK. I think we've/If you could keep us in touch at school with the toilet-training. If there's any way we can help at all, certainly we'll back you up.

DR   We haven't answered (health visitor's) question though have we? Or the (assessment hospital) part.

HT   Yes.

DR   That's what we haven't answered that you er raised previously." - Educational case-conference.

Despite the similar ways in which professional knowledge is made through observation and records, it is clear that there are differences between doctors and psychologists and indeed between different doctors. On occasions when professionals do try to deal with a practical problem, different solutions may be proposed by different professionals. An educational psychologist for example suggests that a mother deals with the problem of her child's incontinence by educating the child to change wet sheets thus reducing the work she has to do.

> EP "I think you know if/That all needs a/You know, needs you to make a bit of, you know/It's you changing your ways a little bit and making/
>
> M   Yes.
>
> EP Rearranging things. And there's the nuisance of having to teach (him) how to do his bed.
>
> M   Yes, yes.
>
> EP And what happens if he, he doesn't make it right or he doesn't do the right things with the wet sheet. But ... in the long run I think you've got to swing it so it's worth his while." - Meeting between Educational psychologist and mother.

The educational psychologist stresses the psychological motivation of the child and involves the mother in an educational role. On the other hand a doctor sees the situation in a strictly physical way and emphasizes technology and the enuresis alarm machine:

> DR "Well I mean you say he can do it if he tries. He's sometimes successful and he's sometimes not. But I think he can't try to be dry when he's asleep. It either happens or it doesn't. And I think it's because of his deep sleep that he doesn't know the signal that the full bladder is there." - Paediatric clinic.

The important point to note, however, is that both alternatives involve the mother in a considerable amount of work, either in working to educate the child or in having sleep-disturbed nights (lifting the child up from bed to take it to the toilet). Now, one of the usual functions of doctors is to provide people with a legitimate excuse for not doing their normal work (Cartwright, 1967, p.46), providing sick notes etc. for those in paid employment. But however sympathetic a doctor may be, 'excusing' a mother her work appears quite ridiculous when there is no obvious alternative person to do it.

> M   "Oh, well he's got the bleep (i.e. enuresis alarm machine) and you've got to keep lifting him all the while. Well I lifted him right up until eleven o'clock at night. The doctor says, oh don't do that, you're making it hard work for yourself. I thought yes, but I said, it's keeping the bed dry and it's easier for me to do." - Meeting between Educational psychologist and mother.

Even crisis help, such as admitting the child to hospital involves the mother in the time and expense of transport. In any case another doctor believes that a period in hospital does not solve incontinence.

> DR   "The thing about enuresis is that it changes/the pattern often can change completely in hospital. Children often just stop wetting. To start again when they go home." - Educational case-conference.

This statement nicely sums up the difficulty of the relationship between professional knowledge and actually helping with practical problems. Professional knowledge is based so much on historical conditions where people have been separated out and made distinct, that the few solutions it proposes fail. They fail because they reproduce the same problem - a considerable amount of work for the mother to deal with. Or they fail because having made ordinary problems into one of the special characteristics of the handicapped (by observing groups separated from other people), and solved the problem in a special way (hospital), the solution does not work because it has to be a solution to an ordinary problem.

(b) Limits to Professional Knowledge

There are definite limits to what can be achieved by professional knowledge based on observing and recording characteristics of the handicapped. As was suggested at the end of the last section, medical knowledge is limited by the very fact of being technical and specialized.

> "The mother said that with his enuresis, the enuresis alarm machine was helping and I recommend this alternate months, and the Triptizol has also helped and I recommend this alternate weeks." - Files: paediatrician.

In the end neither the equipment nor the drugs helped (parental interview) which shows that such specialized knowledge does not necessarily mean that an ordinary problem can be resolved. On the other hand, if knowledge does not necessarily mean that a problem can be controlled, the reverse is also true. Neither the professionals nor the parents seem to be aware that a great deal of valuable and practical help can be given without knowing the exact nature of the problem, or indeed without knowing the cause of a child's disability. If there are limits to what professional knowledge can achieve, then there are equally greater opportunities than are generally realized to help parents by dealing with problems as ordinary difficulties. If professionals are sometimes uncertain what is expected of them by the parents (see Cartwright, 1967, pp. 218-219), then it is probably because they are caught between their specialized technical knowledge (often inappropriate) and being genuinely symphathetic about practical problems without realizing that they are just a more complicated version of everyday problems. In other words the professionals have a social gap in their life-styles which in general exclude them from the everyday experiences of women and the working class. The unfortunate result is that professionals record practical problems in their files which in itself helps to maintain the idea that they are special problems. And speculation about those problems reinforces a misunderstanding which the professionals have, namely that a handicapped child means a handicapped family.

We have seen how specialized professional knowledge is of very limited use when dealing with practical problems. Doctors in particular may see them as trivial issues, and regard it as inappropriate for parents to approach them about such questions (see Cartwright, 1967, pp. 40-41). There is also evidence that patients regard doctors as unsuited to deal with their general problems, but that despite this many would still turn to their doctor to deal with this general problem (Cartwright and Anderson, 1981, pp. 51-52). In this study there are several occasions when a mother raises a general problem (walking, feeding, incontinence) in the paediatric clinic. It may be the case that these are unreasonable demands on the doctors, but it is because the mother is desperate and has nowhere else to turn that she asks. The result is that the doctor insists that these are problems that the mother must deal with by herself by her own hard work. But of course a doctor must be sympathetic and not express this idea so harshly, but kindly suggest this to the mother:

> DR   "But it's worthwhile you doing a bit of work yourself.
>
> M   Yes I will. I'll write to the Down's (Association) and see what they have to say." - Paediatric clinic.

The doctor may also feel pressured in this if he feels the mother is wanting to turn all the responsibility for decision-making to the doctor (see Stimson and Webb, 1975, p. 88). In the following example the problems of a child's walking and feeding are referred to as work for the mother to do. But the doctor also uses the mother's good nature to play down the work by making 'humorous' comments:

> DR   "Needs to put on more weight ... He needs more food.
>
> M   How do I do that? (laughs)
>
> DR   You're to fill him up.

M	I keep filling him up.
DR	Otherwise he should bring next time some rocks in his pocket." - Paediatric clinic.

However, it seems that the doctor can sometimes be more openly sympathetic towards practical problems and talk at length about them. This happens when the problems are potential ones that have not materialized (e.g. the child has learned to walk perfectly well), and the parents do not experience problems about that particular issue (though they might about others). But at the same time it is made clear that the doctor is not acting in his medical role and the conversation is distinguished from strictly medical topics. In other words the doctor involves the parent in some informal polite conversation. To judge from my own experiences of interviewing the parents, when I was aware of involving myself in polite talk, it probably felt too embarrassing to deal with parents simply as objects of research, especially when I had no practical help to offer. And to the extent that doctors are in the same position, they probably feel likewise.

DR	"Are you keeping well? You look all right.
M	Always on the go. (laughs)
DR	Always on the go. I expect you are, you've got a family to run.
M	Yes, busy housewife, go out to work.
DR	You go out to work as well? What do you do?
M	I'm on the health side. Domestic. Up um school dentists there (..)
DR	Ah, that's good.
M	Yes, yes.
DR	School dentist.
M	That's how I get to know about his teeth you see. (laughs)
DR	Yes. That's good. Splendid." - Paediatric clinic.

The fact that this type of informal conversation takes place, and is distinguished from strictly medical questions also affects how a practical problem may be dealt with in the paediatric clinic. In this example the parents and the doctor discuss the problem of a child's sickness which might possibly be linked to a certain type of feeding (whether the child has cow's or goat's milk). During the clinic the parents make two different <u>types</u> of suggestion as to the cause of the sickness. One is that it has to do with the milk feeding. But several other suggestions they make sound more technical and medical (e.g. the child has a blockage, or is vomiting bile or is having complications to hay-fever). The paediatrician treats the two types of suggestion very differently. Any suggestions made by the parents which sound technical or medical, the doctor dismisses by reference to his professional knowledge. But the feeding explanation is allowed to remain a possibility.

> DR "Well, what about trying the goat's milk again?
>
> M Yes.
>
> F She's back on it now.
>
> DR Oh, she is.
>
> M I found this week/
>
> DR And is she better?
>
> F Well she's only been on it two days, so it's too early.
>
> DR Yes, yes.
>
> M But that's it. I was trying to think of all in her diet and that's the only thing I could think of.
>
> DR Yes it could be an allergic reaction. A violent one. That would fit in with goat's milk making it better and cow's milk not/ What else?" - Paediatric clinic.

There seems to be two reasons for this. Firstly, the doctor may feel that a feeding problem is outside medical knowledge and is therefore not required to be dealt with. And secondly if it is not seen as strictly a medical problem then it provides the doctor with a good opportunity to engage in informal polite conversation about it. It therefore releases him from pressure to offer a solution, because he is not acting in his capacity as a representative of all medical knowledge in the sense referred to by Stimson and Webb (1975, p. 51):

> "When asking questions the patient makes reference to the doctor as a representative of medical knowledge rather than asking what the doctor himself can do (...) The doctor in his responses to questions seems not to admit inability to act but refers to the wider body of knowledge which he represents."

However, how much individual doctors actually know falls short of this ideal status that doctors have of being a representative of all medical knowledge. This is especially so in a practical sense as the mother is often the one who has the greatest knowledge about a child. Doctors then probably feel very insecure in their relationship with parents. Indeed, one doctor told me that he found dealing with parents in clinics very stressful (fieldwork diary). As we have already seen, professionals tend to view practical problems as evidence that a child is handicapped. And so a Senior Clinical Medical Officer can say about a child who has a severe hearing impairment:

> DR   "So what is really coming through from this testing and what you've shown me and told me is how handicapped he is on the hearing and speech side." - Visit by Medical officer.

Later in the same meeting the doctor is embarrassed by the mother's greater knowledge and his own ignorance in a situation where typically he is the one who is supposed to have the knowledge and be in control. To save face the doctor changes his explanation to suggest something that a professional would not normally do, namely that a practical problem is responsible for a child's slow progress:

> M   "Um, are you aware that he has a paralysed right vocal chord? None of us were until the nineteenth of May when they operated on his heart. (laughs)
> DR   Oh.
> M   And they said, the E.N.T. people that that would have a lot to do with the

fact he's not talking yet.
DR   I would have thought that the hearing is more../
M   Yes.
DR   Personally.
M   Yes.
DR   I think if you are deaf, you can't hear and therefore you can't respond." - Visit by Medical officer.

A situation where the doctor has to work hard at his relationship with the parent to avoid losing face can hardly make it more easy for the professionals to offer any help to parents with their practical difficulties.

Indeed, the limitations of medical knowledge may even mean that the doctors consciously avoid dealing with the practical problems of the parents. To the paediatrician a practical problem may not only seem trivial, and inappropriate for him to have to deal with, but the whole clinic may seem routine and boring. If most parents report at a routine clinic that the child is progressing (or not) much the same as usual, then the paediatrician may find this relatively uninteresting, even boring, given the number of patients they see. Otherwise the limits to medical knowledge make practical problems seem inappropriate for doctors to deal with and these difficulties are therefore side-stepped. This may mean ignoring the practical dimension of the problem (e.g. what it means to the parents to have disturbed and sleepless nights) and merely recording the medical aspects.

M   "He has a more severe fit now (...) He seems to call out. You know, makes a noise with it. Yes it wakes us. And he never used to.
DR   Have they changed in any other way?" - Paediatric clinic.

Furthermore, if the doctor explains the medical aspect of the problem (for example, how the different drugs that he is giving the child react with one another) he may create the impression that he has also dealt with the practicalities of the problem from the parents' point of view.

M	"Is there anything, you know, like a medium perhaps, to try and help his sleeping?
DR	Mmn-hmn. Mmn ..... I see. Yes, OK. I mean I can give you some/see whether er the amount, you know, would make him fairly sleepy or not. OK.
M	Because we were supposed to have given him one spoonful a night, but we only gave him half a spoonful and still the next day he cried nearly all day. It really does make him feel rotten.
DR	Yes, yes. The thing is he's on this valium one also and this vallergan. Probably they potentiate the reaction.
M	Yes.
DR	So that's why probably he was too sleepy. Anything else?" - Paediatric clinic.

Or else the routine of the clinic, with the doctor pressing on to the next scheduled question, may cause a practical problem (e.g. toileting) to be avoided:

M	"He usually goes each day but it's very hard. He's, you know.
F	Yesterday you had to clear him out.
M	Yesterday I did clear him out myself because he hadn't been the day before and he seemed to have a job to be going.
DR	Aha. Which school does he go to?" - Paediatric clinic.

Either this avoidance is not intentional but a result of letting the routine take over the conversation or else it may be a deliberate strategy if the doctor feels there is a limit to what can be achieved medically. In other contexts doctors may feel that this is the sort of work they can leave to nurses. Of course in some instances where there are limits to what medicine can do there are other professionals who could offer practical help to whom the doctors could refer parents and child. For example, one paediatrician suggests a referral to the occupational therapy department. But in fact the mother concerned told me three months later that nothing had come of the proposal. She thought the suggestion had been 'a show' put on for my benefit as a researcher (fieldwork diary). Certainly my presence in the clinic may have been a reminder to the doctor that medicine is unsuited to deal with practical problems, with the result that the unkept promise was made. The limits to medical knowledge and practice also lead the doctors to seize desperately on what few aspects of a problem they can deal with. The heart condition of, say, a Down's Syndrome child may be the one medical aspect of development that could be life-threatening. The desire to make certain that what little can be done is done, and perhaps fearing what trouble he might find himself in if it is not, leads this doctor to interrupt other problems the mother wants to put forward:

DR	"OK. Any problems?
M	Not really she/
DR	Particularly heart problems first thing.
M	No. not at the moment she/
DR	OK. Absolutely OK. Right ...."
	- Paediatric clinic.

(c)   What Professionals Expect of the Parents

We have noted that professionals see it as a responsibility of the parents to deal with practical problems. On the other hand this responsibility is not regarded as work. It is clear, for example, that when what professionals expect to have happened has not, then it is regarded as an inconvenience for the services who are not prepared (in either sense of the word) to deal with the problem.

> "Refused admission to primary school because of enuresis and soiling." - Files: Medical officer.

It is these expectations that professionals have of parents - to have their child toilet-trained by a certain age. But such expectations, when recorded in professional files, can inadvertently portray the concerned mother as over-anxious or, worse, as a troublemaker. On the one hand it is seen as quite acceptable for school placement to be affected if a practical problem is experienced by the services.

> "The actual school to be used, I think, must be left to the Education Department depending upon transport availability." - Files: Medical officer.

But this is not the case if the practical problem is experienced by the mother:

> "It appears that X is becoming a problem at home and mother is finding it very difficult to cope. Mother feels that X's behaviour would improve if she went to (ESN(M) school)." - Files: Educational Welfare Officer.

> "X is appropriately placed at (ESN(S) school) and Mrs. X will be visited and discussions held to this effect." - Files: Educational Psychologist.

The expectation that various practical difficulties must be dealt with by further work by the parents (especially the mother) is reinforced in a number of ways. It may be that professionals hope for gratitude from the parents as part of the 'rewarding' nature of their work. In this case the fact that a mother will take on extra work to help, say, her child improve its communication, is interpreted simply as the mother being grateful. She may well be grateful, but she is also taking on a great deal of extra work. And work it most certainly is, however much the professionals (and indeed the mother) may see it as natural mothering.

> ST   "So um, her mother has learned some of the early stages of Maketon (sign language). And I've been over to their home. And they're quite keen to carry on using that at home. Which is very nice. I've had a nice bit of contact there." Educational case-conference.

Another reason that work tends not to be recognized as such, is that involving parents closely with work done at school is seen as a special privilege, as this is not usually what happens in other schools. In fact extra work comes to be something that is seen as an appropriate part of what it means to be a parent of a disabled child.

HT   "The set of objectives is to get him →
T   His arms.
HT   To straighten his arms. Can that also be shared with home? I'm sure that mum and dad will →
T   Yes I'm going to/
HT   Work on that area." - Educational case-conference.

This expectation of the professionals that parents must do more work is strengthened by the fact that the professionals regard themselves as a scarce resource with restrictions on their time which must be shared with many children:

T   "He homes in with it, and he definitely gets there sometimes/ I think with intensive physiotherapy he could, I really do ..... that one arm. It's the right one.
EP   And obviously, you know, it's got to be balanced against the time you spend/ I mean obviously we've spent an awful lot of time with him this morning, but, you know, as a regular thing that's clearly not on." - Meeting between Teacher and Educational Psychologist.

In this way parents will do the work because they realize no-one else will, and the feeling that this work is part of what parents should normally be expected to do is reinforced. But expecting the parents to do extra work to deal with practical problems has unfortunate consequences. And one of these is that if practical problems such as sleeping and incontinence persist then the professionals tend to blame the continuing problems on the way the parents are managing the child. To an outside observer the professionals then seem to be making damaging moral judgements about the parents. Often the parents will not know these comments are being made and will have no opportunity to challenge their validity.

EP   "The difference is, in school you <u>can't</u> give him your attention. I mean he's working within the constraints of being at school. He can't get all your attention.

> Whereas at home, perhaps, he's got enough muscle, enough leverage over mum and dad." - Meeting between Teacher and Educational Psychologist.

What is true in the case of professional meetings where parents are not present is equally true of the files. The professionals make recommendations in the files (and this does not necessarily mean that they are explained to the parents) about how a child ought to be managed to overcome a practical problem, and follow it with a statement expecting the parents to act in this way.

> "The boy is hyperactive and requires firm management." - Files: Medical officer.

By doing this the professionals are creating a situation where they have to judge the parents. If the problem is not resolved it may then appear that the parents have not done enough extra work or not listened to the recommendations of the professionals. The professional help, based on separating the experiences of a mentally-handicapped child from ordinary problems, depends on expecting the mother to do all this work without acknowledging it in any way. If the professionals anticipate that this expected work will not be done, then they make social judgements for which they are not qualified, let alone accountable. It is because the work that mothers do is not usually recognized that when faced with the possibility that it is not done, the professionals then make moral judgements about how near a mother comes to achieving an impossibly high workload.

> "X looks very well cared for. I believe this coincides with the greater involvement by her grandparents in her care. What does concern me is the possibility of X's mother getting a house of her own and taking X with her. Should that happen then X's progress will need to be carefully monitored." - Files: Doctor.

This is one way in which caring professionals contribute to social prejudice in general. Because many such instances will be recorded in medical, psychological, social work and educational files, the professionals will come to see one-parent families as a social problem <u>in themselves</u> and talk about 'one-parent family situation' and 'social problem - divorced parents' - Files: Paediatrician. It is precisely at the moment when professionals think they are being most sensitive to social issues that they are most patronizing, most morally damaging and contribute most to the unwarranted stigma that divorced or single parents are subject to.

But perhaps the most important part of the work that professionals expect parents to do is to attend meetings with them, especially clinics. We have already seen how and why the professionals do not deal with practical problems. Of course the mother may not tell a doctor, for example, about various practical problems because she may already feel that he may find them trivial and cannot be dealt with by his professional knowledge. She may even stop attending the clinic with the child. Meanwhile the doctor may not realize that just by the fact of seeing the mother and child he is not giving any practical help. Or he may not know what to do to help. In this case regular check-ups may be the only thing he can offer, though this might be an inconvenience for mother and child. But with this expectation that the mother should at least turn up to receive the minimal help he can give (a routine review), if she does not then she is thought of as a bad parent and moral judgements are recorded in the files:

> "Mrs. X is apparently distraught because of X's behaviour and feels that nobody is interested in her problems or taking any notice of her. Nevertheless, she phoned to cancel her appointment today - this is the second cancelled appointment. When she is interested I will arrange to see her myself next time." - Files: Paediatrician.

However, in extreme cases the professionals do apparently recognize that mothers are faced with extra work.

> " ... the mother has doubts about her capacity to manage a handicapped child in addition to her four normal present children." - Files: Doctor.

If fact it might be suggested that in such cases the extreme burden of work was a major contribution in deciding whether a child could be brought up at home or had to be left in hospital. But whilst the "legitimation of patients' exemption from normal social responsibilities is traditionally one of the accepted functions of the patient's doctor" (Cartwright, 1967, p. 46), even if the doctors wanted to excuse a mother this heavy workload there is no-one else to do it.

> "Mrs. X's anxiety (is) about being unable to look after him virtually on her own due to her husband having to work shifts." - Files: Social worker.

Judging from the disapproving reaction of professionals when a mentally-handicapped child is not brought up in the so-called 'natural' family, professionals expect families to remain together. What families bringing up a handicapped child do can be explained as a perfectly normal response to an extremely heavy workload dealing with a more complicated version of normal practical problems. But by expecting a family to be able to cope with this work (sometimes not realizing that it is work) and expecting the family to be kept together (knowing only too well the depressing prospect of growing up on a hospital ward) leads the professionals into monitoring how the families cope.

> "Caring for, and working with X undoubtedly involves Mr. and Mrs. X in a considerable expenditure of time and energy, but this does not seem to have been at the expense of their contact with the local community or of their family life." - Files: Educational Psychologist (his/her emphasis).

> "There seems to be some tensions in the home. Bruising has been noted." - Files: Assessment Unit.

Once again the consequence is damaging moral evaluations. In the second of these two extracts it is unfounded speculation which the parents cannot challenge because they are not allowed to see the files. The real danger is that it becomes believable as a 'fact' simply by virtue of being recorded in a professional file. Given also the powers of authorities to take children into care this could have serious consequences. Once again it is ironic that in trying to be sensitive to social problems (non-accidental injury) the professional has libelled the parents and possibly put a child's future at risk.

If the professionals expect parents to do certain types of work to solve their practical problems, then they also expect the parents to give up their responsibility for making their own decisions. When parents meet doctors, for example, the doctors may expect the parents to put themselves and their child entirely in the hands of the doctor (to develop Stimson and Webb, 1975, p. 88). In fact each individual parent will vary in how much responsibility they want to give up: some think that doctors know best, others question everything that is told to them (interviews with parents). There is little doubt that doctors think they know best, and they expect that part of their job will be to get the parent to accept their view of things, for fear that the course of action they recommend will not be followed (to develop Stimson and Webb, 1975, p. 81). It is easy to understand why the doctors would soon lose face if their advice was rarely taken. But it is also easy to understand the difficulties that this creates for the parents. On the one hand there is not much the professionals can do with regard to their practical problems. But on the other hand they want the parents to accept their view of the child which of course involves seeing any problems as special and distinctive and part of what it means to have the condition 'mental handicap'. This then means that doctors will regard certain types of help as appropriate and will encourage them.

> "She was previously a physiotherapist at the (assessment hospital) and has had considerable experience in dealing with brain-damaged children. She is now building up a private practice in (town) and I am sure she would be able to give Mr. and Mrs. X considerable help." - Files: Medical officer.

But other types of help will be discouraged because they are seen as inappropriate:

> " ... spent time and money on the Doman Delacato regime." - Files: Doctor.

These professional expectations have a number of

consequences, leading the professionals to reinforce certain political and social prejudices as well as to make moral evaluations of the parents. There are important political consequences of the concern of the professionals for the child's welfare that shows itself in the belief that the child is necessarily best off in its own home. By approving attempts to solve the huge burden of extra work by turning to one's own family the professionals are helping to maintain a myth that such help from relatives (and friends and neighbours) is widely and generally available to mothers of mentally-handicapped children.

> "Mrs. X's parents have moved into an extension built onto the house and with such support she copes extremely well with X's needs." - Files: Educational Psychologist.

But this help is not widely available. Mothers of severely mentally-handicapped children receive only minimal help from husbands let alone other relatives, friends or neighbours (D. Wilkin, 1979). But by helping to maintain this myth, the professionals help those policy-makers who like to appeal to the virtues of independence and self-help, leaving many families dependent on the crisis-help of phased-care when the pressure of work becomes too much.

> ".. I think the family are having great difficulties in managing her. It seems to me that a break every now and again would be best for them all." - Files: Doctor.

Professional concern for the welfare of the child can also become a means of re-affirming the social prejudices which limit the range of social activities available to families of the mentally-handicapped. The message implicit from reading the following two comments seems to be that families with a mentally-handicapped child are a handicapped family and must take handicapped holidays.

> "However, his mother is now very happy to let him go to school (.....) I believe her change of heart came about when she was persuaded to leave X in a Children's Home while the family had a holiday within the ambit of phased-care,

> which, as you know, the Social Services are managing to provide most of our parents with very handicapped children." - Files: Educational Psychologist.

> "I quite agree with you that a holiday (abroad) with mother and her friends would not be a good idea for X." - Files: Doctor.

As has already been argued, such practical problems as taking holidays or the mother having paid employment exist anyway for mothers of young children because of the structure and attitudes of our society. Paid employment for mothers is a problem because it is sometimes a necessity to survive and often a basic right denied through lack of creche or nursery provision. Paid employment for mothers becomes, for the professionals, another measure of how much they have persuaded parents to the professional point of view, and becomes a moral judgement on them.

> "Socially the mother seems to be well and is probably better off for having a job in the evenings." - Files: Doctor.

The matter is made more difficult for the mothers if the professional viewpoints are not consistent.

> "Her mother works during the day and all three adults look after X as best they can. This always produces a great strain on all concerned." - Files: Doctor.

In the long term the expectations that professionals have of parents which lead to these judgements leave the parents confused and frustrated.

> F   "When we tried to help X ourselves and pay out of our own pocket privately they said you shouldn't do that. I said why? (...) They said you're throwing (money) away. You'd be better off to put that (money) to find out what's wrong with the children (i.e. medical research). Oh dear, you try to help your own child and you get condemned for that.

M   And ever since then you're getting very
         funny looks (...) You mustn't go against
         the system." - Interview with parents.

(d) How Relationships between Professionals and
     Parents are Managed

We have already seen how professionals, especially doctors, try to get the parents to accept the professionals' view of the child, because they want the parents to follow their recommendations. We have also seen how this can lead to professionals morally judging the parents depending on how close they come to arranging their lives in the way the professionals think is best. Many mothers seem somehow aware of this and consequently, where possible, will attempt to show that a certain problem is not really a difficulty for them (as indeed it may not be). Firstly, this may mean demonstrating how they have certain difficulties under control and they can cope with their family routine. In this example a mother shows how a practical issue over transport fits neatly into the family routine. The mother makes sure her pleasure (that school transport arrangements coincide now her child is transferring to the same school as his brother) is known.

M   "And the transport I see every morning
         when I take (sister) on the playbus. It's
         (name of bus company)
EP   Well if it's fixed up for (brother) then X
         just gets on with him.
M   Well this is it. They can both get on
         together. Yeh." - Meeting between
         Educational Psychologist and Mother.

Secondly, the mother may attempt to show how a 'normal' family life is being achieved (Voysey, 1975), and also indicate ways in which the child behaves 'normally'. This may be part of a general strategy to treat the child, and get others to treat the child, as normally as possible (F. Davis, 1963).

DR   "She's pretty happy?
M   Um yes .... very contented.
DR   She is. So from the point of view of
         behaviour you don't have any difficulties?

M	Not really. She's a little bit annoying when she gets a bit bored because she makes an erring noise then.
DR	Does she?
M	But I think it's something that's just with boredom.
DR	Yes.
M	And um I don't think it's a sort of trying to communicate. It's a sort of different noise to that.
X	Errrh.
DR	What, that one we've just heard there?
M	Oh, no. That was the protesting one (laughs)
DR	Oh, I see.
M	She doesn't do it very often." - Paediatric clinic.

Thirdly, the mother may feel she has to show not only how certain practical issues are under control, but also that she is as self-reliant as possible (not a burden on the Welfare State), is acting in a responsible way that professionals would see as appropriate and has a 'balanced' view of the problems.

DR	"That old wheelchair is still going is it?
M	Yes it's very good actually .... we've got someone else's now.
DR	Have you?
M	Yes (laughs) .. well there's no alternative for in the car is there?
DR	No.
M	I mean they're not safe to lay on the back seat.
DR	No." Paediatric clinic.

If to avoid being badly thought of the parents stress how certain practicalities (transport, communication, behaviour, mobility) are not really problems, then this may tend to confirm to professionals that there is little that they can do, or worse, that it is therefore reasonable to assume that other mothers can cope. Such is the trail of consequences that stems from professionals trying to get parents to accept their point of view. But in getting parents to accept their view of things, professionals may also offer a service that parents do not really want. In this example the parents are receiving informal help from a small-scale community hospital to deal with the problem of sleeping. The doctor wants the parents to use the official 'shared-care' provision at the assessment hospital. Some other parents are not happy with such an arrangement because they have an aversion to leaving their child in a large-scale institution or because their child reacts badly to being in such a hospital. The parents in this case make clear the benefit they get from the small community hospital, but the doctor tries to persuade the parents to see the facilities he wants to see used as appropriate.

M	"I was finding very helpful with (community hospital) was just to be able to ring up when I was desperate and say, oh, can you have him for a couple of nights? 'Cause he doesn't sleep. But since he's been in this last week/Well I don't know whether he slept or not but he hasn't got us out of bed. He's been/we have slept through the night.
F	We/We've had probably our best <u>week's</u> sleep.
(M	That we've had, oh, for years I should
(	think.
(F	Oh for years, yes.
	(....)
DR	Now/Certainly a lot of parents from children at (ESN(S) school) do find it helpful if they do have a regular break.
M	Yes.
DR	What we would call 'phased-care'.
M	Yes.
DR	That you would make a/what should we say, a contract, or an agreement with ..... per/a hospital/probably (assessment hospital)." - Visit by Medical Officer.

If, as has already been suggested, the parents try hard not to upset the professionals in any way then this may make parents reluctant to speak up for themselves:

M	"... but I didn't want/my name being Mrs.

X/I thought if ever I needed them it could go down that, you know, 'That's that Mrs. X'. So I thought X might suffer." - Interview with parents.

M   "But I still keep in with the hospital because you've got to. You've got to keep in with the hospital because you don't know when you're going to need them for anything really." - Interview with parents.

Consequently it is easy to see why parents feel pressured to accept (and accept gratefully at that) services that they do not feel to be particularly helpful.

(e) How Relationships with Other Professionals are
     Managed
It has already been argued how, in trying to be good professionals and getting parents to accept their point of view, professionals can end up offering unhelpful services. But there may be other types of pressures which reinforce the ways in which the professionals allocate these services. To return to an example already used, a doctor may try to persuade parents to use the 'phased-care' scheme at the assessment hospital. But the doctor is also part of a bureaucracy and may have administrative as well as medical or practical responsibilities. In fact during the study a Senior Clinical Medical Officer remarked how the administrative side of his job was now greater than the medical side (fieldwork diary). Certainly to an outside observer an important aspect of the Senior Clinical Medical Officer's job is the efficient administration of services. This means that he must deal with the services that are available - he cannot will appropriate services into existence. Furthermore, informal services which are felt by the parents to be appropriate (such as the community hospital) may be outside his jurisdiction. And sticking closely to the official resources is the best means of ensuring that he acts fairly and that he does not give preference to rich parents, or parents whom he likes personally. And so both self-inspired professionalism and bureaucratic need may persuade parents to use a service which will involve the parents in all the practical

problems of their child being in a large-scale hospital.

> DR   "Within the hospital they are in small wards, where there are trained staff, where they can do things. There is a school attached to the hospital and during a child's time within (assessment hospital) they can go to school. So they're not going to miss out.
>
> M   No.
>
> DR   On their schooling ... Obviously they would be very happy for you to see the place, go and meet it, see the staff and see what you think of it." - Visit by Medical officer.

To an outside observer it can begin to seem as if the doctor is putting the provision of clients for a hospital before the real needs of parents and child.

A not dissimilar explanation can be made of how the best interests of the child may take second place to certain relationships between professionals. A junior hospital doctor may feel a lack of esteem relative to hospital consultants (to develop Cartwright, 1967, p. 141), especially consultants who are in specialities other than paediatrics. No doubt from the point of view of the junior doctor, some of his unwritten training is in having to learn that part of what it means to be a professional is being able to make decisions without outside interference. So when a mother asks for help in sorting out a problem over the child's communication and hearing aids, the doctor avoids the issue by appealing to the fact that he is expected to act in a certain way by other doctors.

> M   "But because of his deafness.
>
> DR   Mnn.
>
> M   It's a real problem ..... getting through to him.
>
> DR   Mmn .... Mmn ..... So (the hearing specialist) is going to look at him to/
>
> M   He's seeing him Thursday afternoon, yes. So um .... I don't know whether you can make/recommend anything as well or whether it's just him.
>
> DR   Once (hearing specialist) is involved, I

```
                    think perhaps no. Because he doesn't like
                    er
(                   some people telling him what to do and
(                   other things. He says, I'm expected to do
(                   my job, so let me do my job
(M                  No I think this is ........................
(                   yes, yes.
  DR                I've been in trouble sometimes in the
                    past.
  M                 Oh, I see (laughs)
  DR                So now I will not enter in that field.
  M                 No, no." - Paediatric clinic.
```

But this unwillingness to criticize other professionals, or
to modify their advice, even when to do so would benefit
the child, means that some of the practical problems that
mother and child have will remain unresolved. In the long
term this might mean that respect for doctors will
diminish if the concern to protect themselves from abuse
and exploitation means incompetence or unhelpfulness is
protected.

This unwillingness to criticize members of one's own
profession may be matched by a tendency not to criticize
any of the other professionals one is working with. In fact
two psychologists told me that in multi-disciplinary
case-conferences the clinical medical officers were the
professionals who 'smoothed things over' (fieldwork diary).
This is understandable as a Senior Clinical Medical Officer
forms a link between doctors and both teachers and
educational psychologists, and has both hospital-based and
community-based concerns. The Senior Clinical Medical
Officer can therefore play an important role in
maintaining overall professional power by making sure a
united front is given to the parents. One consequence of
this, however, is that they can listen to the parents' point
of view and say they agree whilst at the same time
reinterpreting what has been said. The result is that the
actual viewpoint of the parent never reaches the relevant
professionals. Here a mother puts forward a whole range
of explanations to show why her child attending hospital
for an assessment would cause difficulties. The mother did
not want the child to go to the assessment hospital; the
child had already been once; all the tests had been done
before; the child reacts badly to hospitals; school-teachers
not hospital staff were the best people to assess the child;
the child had had enough interruptions; the child had

recently been disturbed again by an operation. All these are accounts of how being in hospital creates problems, but the doctor's reply suggests that none of the staff at the hospital will be confronted with these accounts:

> DR "Yes, I quite agree with you. So, you know, if the name comes forward again, they will ask me, and I will say that in my opinion he is making steady progress and there is no point in re-assessing him at the unit at present." - Visit by medical officer.

When, in a paediatric clinic, a mother gives a similar account of her child's general dislike of hospitals to explain that she does not want phased-care at the assessment hospital, the paediatrician changes the emphasis of what she says. And he concludes that the child will not be going to the assessment hospital because he feels that a diagnosis of the child's condition is not likely to emerge when so many professionals had seen him already. In both cases the doctors are no doubt trying to maintain good working relationships with the professionals at the assessment hospital with whom they deal. But the consequences may be that the professionals there never come to understand why their service is not always appropriate and the extent of unease about it that exists. The criticism that Oswin (1982) makes about professional relationships within long-stay hospitals (namely, that professionals will not risk damaging their relationships with one another by making criticisms) seems also to apply to relationships between professionals in such hospitals and those outside.

> "... how much will professionals shut their eyes to in the interests of preserving 'good relationships', and when do professional responsibilities towards the children have to take priority over good relationships?" (Oswin, 1982, p. 318)

This unwillingness to criticize other professionals and what they do is another factor which may create pressure to make use of services which are there, irrespective of whether or not they are sometimes inappropriate or create practical problems from the parents' point of view. In other words, not to refer parents and child to an existing service would be seen as an insult or an attack on that service. In this example, in his eagerness to persuade both himself and the parents about what should be done a doctor misunderstands the exact nature of the practical problem:

	"(the child is babbling and crying loudly)
DR	Oh, no. You were ever so quiet, weren't you? (M laughs)
M	(to child) ...... Do you want to do this?
DR	But this is the problem you get. That he starts off, I suppose. And then you feel .....
M	And then I go around nearly all day trying to find out what he does want (laughs)
DR	Yes.
M	By the end of the day we're screaming at each other.
DR	Yes.
M	Yes. It's very frustrating isn't it X?" - Visit by Medical officer.

The doctor has understood the problem to be about the very fact that the child is crying and the irritation this must surely cause the mother, who must therefore be in need of a break (hence the persuasion to have phased-care). But the mother appears to be saying that the root of the problem is communication. The child's crying is a symptom of the frustration it feels because it cannot communicate to the mother what it wants.

The powerlessness that doctors and other professionals feel may be judged from corresponding comments in their files - times when they appear to have understood the practical problems of the parents. There is little they can do individually to change the existing services, even when the practical problems caused for parents and child by being in hospital are realized by professionals in the community:

"I am a little concerned about the possibility of regression if a long inpatient assessment at (hospital) is envisaged. I know a great deal of valuable information would be gained, but there

> is some evidence that X reacts adversely to hospitalization ..." - Files: Educational Psychologist.

But at the same time there is no easy way to transfer hospital funds to community care which would retain job security for the various hospital-based professionals. Consequently there are continuing anxieties and dilemmas both for the parents and for the professionals.

> "The mother seems to be managing fairly well and if some short periods of relief care are needed I will see what I can do but the mother is very keen to avoid hospital admissions." - Files: Assessment Unit.

CONCLUSION

From what has been written it should be clear that the parents, especially the mothers, are involved in a great deal of unpaid work in dealing with the practical problems of bringing up their children. The problems reported are very similar to those in other studies that have looked at physically disabled, mentally-handicapped or ESN(S) children. The problems are the ordinary problems of bringing up children only complicated and extended over many more years.

The way in which professional knowledge has developed has looked at the mentally-handicapped as a special and distinctive group which has had important political consequences. Firstly, this means that other social groups (the poor, the unemployed, slow-learners) can be blamed by the dominant classes for their own ordinary problems. Secondly, there is little in professional knowledge which enables them to offer practical solutions to the parents. Thirdly, in recording the special characteristics of the mentally-handicapped (as a means of doing what little they can) the professionals incorporate unnecessary social judgements. These artificially reduce the child's social world, and also morally judge the parents depending upon whether the parents have brought the child up in a way in which the professionals think they should have done. Finally, the different professional viewpoint on handicap that therefore emerges makes it increasingly difficult for the professionals to understand the practical problems. Where their concern does suggest solutions it involves the parents in even greater work, or fails because it is a special solution to an ordinary problem.

Professionals and parents do not always realize that help can sometimes be provided without knowing the diagnosis and that the diagnosis does not necessarily suggest what help can be given. Doctors in particular may feel practical problems to be trivial, inappropriate - even routine and boring. They may therefore ignore or avoid dealing with such problems. Or they may stress only the medical aspects with the result that sometimes they do not even become aware of the practical dimensions. Solutions are offered as sympathetic commonsense observers, not as medical representatives.

Work that parents, especially mothers, do in bringing up children is not generally acknowledged. And as professionals make special characteristics out of ordinary problems, they come to expect parents of handicapped children to do special amounts of work. If the practical problem endures, then the way is open to blaming the way the parents have handled the child. Meanwhile other social issues affect the amount of work mothers do with regard to their handicapped child, come to reinforce social prejudices against single, working or divorced mothers. Expecting the family to keep together and to do all this work, when all the professionals can really do is keep an eye on things, leads to more value-judgements, especially about how and where parents seek help.

To professionals it is therefore important to get parents to accept their view of things. If the parents realize this they will not want to offend the professionals. They will play down their problems or not tell the professionals at all. They will show how well they can cope and appear to be grateful for services which they sometimes do not want.

Meanwhile professionals may press parents to accept services which do not solve practical problems because of bureaucratic or administrative considerations, because their livelihood and the maintenance of good working relationships is at stake. If mothers explain to a professional why the services do not always match the practical problems, the professional will not relay the information for the same reasons. In fact eagerness to persuade may mean the professional misunderstands the practical problem in the first place.

If the professionals seem inappropriately matched to the practical problems it is perhaps because only the parents themselves can really solve the difficulties. What they need are more resources that they themselves can control. These include better information, particularly open access to files on their children. More time to solve their own problems by disengaging from services which are not helping, however well-meaning. A greater body of knowledge and a mutual support system by establishing their own self-help parents group. This would increase confidence and self-belief in the social value of the work they do. Finally, and most difficult, these groups would need money, though there is no reason why such groups should not be eligible for money from local authorities or national government.

Chapter Four

PROBLEMS WITH THE SERVICES

PROBLEMS WITH THE SERVICES: INTERVIEWS WITH PARENTS

There are three major themes which emerge as concerning the parents about their relationships with the services. Firstly, on account of certain routines, procedures and availability, resources which could be used to help are not. Next, parents sometimes feel their time and energy is reduced by dealing with services which they do not feel are helping. Finally, as a logical extension of these first two points is the idea that the services systematically detract from the possibility of parents to control their own lives.

(a) Parents Not Listened To
Many of the parents complained that the GP was unable to identify the possibility of a handicapping condition, or indeed did not even listen to the worries expressed by the parents. Similarly, several of the parents felt that paediatricians did not listen to their anxieties or treat them seriously enough in the first instance:

> M   "And it was all hidden under the carpet really, wasn't it? When we faced doctors; I mean when she was eighteen months old we were going to the hospital and my husband turned round to the doctor and said, look (....) what is wrong with my daughter because she's not pulling herself

up properly (....) And she's not doing the things that she should do (....) And he turned round and said, don't <u>worry</u> about it. We have children here of four and they're perfectly normal.

F   'She's a bit backward. She'll catch up in her own time.'

M   And all this was hidden from us."

In view of the many different ways in which the doctors apparently do not listen to the parents, it is interesting that three of the parents reported the doctors as saying that they should listen more to parents, or even that their training taught them to do so. Evidently the training has not been sufficient to overcome the problem.

(b)   <u>Obtaining Information</u>
As far as receiving information from the GP was concerned, two parents expressed pleasure that they had been kept well-informed, whereas a different two complained that information had been kept from them.

M   "(Paediatrician) had a copy of the report and our doctor did. Our doctor's very good actually. He doesn't hide things from you. He'll tell you."

M   "I said to him then, is X a mongoloid baby? And he says, oh, he says, you have noticed something then. I says, yes, I says, but I just couldn't believe that nobody could tell me."

As with GPs there was considerable variation in the quality of information parents felt they received from health visitors. Two parents were thankful for information that the health visitor had passed on, but others felt that for one reason or another the health visitor had not kept them well-informed (as discussed in chapter 5, page 129).

M   "If I was worried or anything I just used to tell the health visitor and she used to get in touch with (GP) and he'd sort of discuss it between themselves, and then she'd used to come back and tell me."

The majority felt that the paediatricians and other hospital-based doctors had not confided in them. The manner in which parents feel that paediatricians' suspicions and important information had been kept from them is dealt with further in the next chapter (p. 127). When such doctors do give some information to the parents, several parents complained that the explanations they were given were in jargon that could not be understood or else they were incomplete or not made sufficiently clear:

> M "He's seen (paediatrician) ever since he was a baby and we didn't know whether it was a lack of oxygen what's made him brain-damaged or what. I mean no-one's actually turned round and said: oh yes, Mrs. X, it was a lack of oxygen to the brain, or anything. We don't really know what's caused his handicap, no-one's told us anything."

Several of the parents also said that sometimes the circumstances made them forget what the doctor had said, or what they wanted to say to the doctor, and that the doctors did not seem to be very sympathetic about these circumstances.

> M "When you've got X sitting with you, X's kind of talking to you or yelling or something in your ear. Being a right nuisance of himself and this doctor's trying to tell you something (...) And you're trying to kind of/got one ear to him and one ear to X, and watching X to see that he doesn't do anything wrong. Cause I have piles of paper and I dread going in there. And you're trying to hold X's hands down so he doesn't get these papers, and listen to the doctors (....) But if you say, well can you speak up a bit, I can't hear you because X is .../ They look at you gone out."

With regard to the doctors and other professionals based at the assessment unit and hospital, many parents felt aggrieved at their exclusion from all or part of the case-conferences held at the end of each assessment, or at not seeing the written report from the assessment. Communication of basic information was again what seemed to concern the parents most about the service offered by the medical officer. A few pointed out that the visit by the medical officer was the first that they knew about special schools. Others were unsure whether the medical officer still saw their child at school, and several felt that it had not been explained to them why the medical officer had never visited or did not visit any more. Although educational psychologists are part of the official procedure for referring children to special schools, only about half the parents thought that their child had been seen at all by an educational psychologist. Many either did not know or were not told if an educational psychologist had seen their child at the ESN(S) school.

> M   "There's a chap goes into school but I don't think he actually/I don't know if he actually sees X at all or .... he's often in the class but it's never been sort of mentioned to me that he's come to see X."

Furthermore, a few parents were simply unsure who, or what, an educational psychologist was. Several parents appreciated the counselling, information or help that they had been given by the social workers.

> F   "Well they put a social worker onto us once we'd got onto the bandwagon as it were (....) She was only really there to help us out with ... nappies and other bits and pieces that were needed. And to give us some advice on what we/what kind of things were available to us, you know. (....)
>
> M   As I say, you know, we've been very satisfied with them. You know, they've been really good."

Finally, a few parents felt that at some point there

had been a breakdown in communication between school and other services:

> SMD   "Has the educational psychologist ever seen X to your knowledge?
>
> M   I don't/We've never had one come here but I think they may have seen him at school. But I've never actually spoken to any that have seen X.
>
> F   We don't know that he's seen one at school.
>
> M   No, but I think a lot of these people are going into school and they do see them."

This leads us to a more detailed consideration of the dependence of parents on being referred from one service to another.

(c)   Dependence for Referral

Just under half the parents said that the GP had been of some help referring their child to other services (medical or otherwise) though two parents were unhappy because they felt that the GP had been obstructive and not given them a way in to other services, particularly hospital specialists:

> F   "You see the thing is with the local GPs and that, they're very cautious of children like X because they don't know a lot about them really you know. Every day they don't deal with a spina bifida child, so that they have to be a bit more cautious. So that normally if there's anything they're worried about they send him down to the general hospital, you know, where they can do further tests. They're pretty good that way, you know. 'Cause I mean obviously they don't deal with a child like him every day. You know. There's things I suppose they're not going to know that a specialist does."
>
> M   "And we took him down, went into the surgery. Had a quick look in his ears, a

quick look down his throat. And he said
there's nothing wrong with him. There's
no sign of any infection. So I said he
doesn't normally lay here like this. You
know, I said, he's normally very active
(...) He wasn't going to refer us to
anybody. So we came out of there very
upset, and decided to take it on our own
back and take him straight up the
hospital. Which after that experience I
would never go to a GP first again."

One mother suggested that a health visitor had
delayed the possibility of a diagnosis, whilst another felt
that the concern shown by the health visitor had speeded
the possibility of a diagnosis. Indeed, one of the practices
of the health visitors that met with parents' approval was
that the health visitors would sometimes put them in
touch with other services. A number of parents expressed
such a view, though others complained that the health
visitor had delayed referring them to other services.

Two parents complained that the recommendations
made by the professionals at the assessment unit had not
been followed up:

F   "But things that came from the assessment,
        ideas that came from it, weren't put into
        practice until we'd done it a lot later.
        We just found that nothing was being
        done. (......) And this is, sort of, what,
        five months after the assessment. And so
        one wonders if we hadn't gone back to
        our own doctor or phoned the (head
        teacher) we still wouldn't have had the
        appointment (....) and we still wouldn't
        have resolved the problem."

In particular two parents were critical that the
psychologists had not passed on information adequately or
not followed up proposals:

M   "(Educational psychologist) was going to
        give (teacher) a programme to do with X.
        And he was going to see that X did it,
        and he was going to see that it was kept

up and one thing and another. And I
haven't heard from him since. So whether
he still goes or what he still does I don't
know."

In this research over a quarter of the parents were
critical of the social services for not having been in
contact, though to be fair one of the complaints of the
social workers themselves is the refusal of the medical
profession to refer cases to them:

F   "But if you say local social services, no,
never helped in any way at all have they
really?

M   No.

F   Unless you actually go down and plead or
ask, and beg for some sort of help. It's
quite a sore point actually. Because as I
say they've started coming this week.
And I consider - she's nearly ten years
old - I think it's a bit late, you know."

(d)   Lack of Services Found Most Helpful
The social workers in the area studied had recently
introduced series of group meetings for parents of
handicapped children (to inform them of the services and
their welfare rights) and all three parents from this group
of twenty who had been involved in such meetings claimed
to have benefitted from them. These series of meetings
were far from being comprehensive, and had all but
ceased when one social worker moved jobs and was not
replaced.

Seven parents had some link with an occupational
therapist and of these, six reported having received some
form of positive help:

F   "I think all the occupational therapists
are first class.

M   They are. They're very good. I think the
thing is they know/if they feel you're
coping they'll leave you alone, but you
know if you need to get in touch with
them you can."

Two parents were disappointed by some aspect of the occupational therapy service, but in such a way as to demonstrate how vital the practical help is that occupational therapists are able to give. It seems ironic that therapists who, as the parents themselves say, are a good source of practical help and advice, are subordinate to professionals who the parents do not feel have such advice or help.

M   "I asked for a standing frame. And the occupational therapist came and she said, yes you can put in for one (.....) We never heard anything about it, and I asked again. And she said, oh I cancelled it, when he went to the (assessment hospital) they said, oh no that wouldn't do him any good at all. Well I know he would because I'm with him all day and I know better than they do. It would have strengthened them because he loved to be on his legs. (....) I got on and on at her and I said he does need it. So apparently she has put in for it again. But he got so heavy I couldn't hold him any more and now when you do it won't push his legs up. Whereas we're sure if he'd had that frame, his little legs would have been a lot stronger than they are now."

This unrealized potential of occupational therapy goes some way to explaining why six of the seven parents still felt that the help that occupational therapy could provide for their child was worthwhile. Moreover, five parents mentioned that their child had been seen by a speech therapist, of whom four had received good practical help or advice, and three thought that their child would continue to benefit if speech therapy were maintained. For this particular group of 20 parents, the issue of physiotherapy provision for their children had become quite symbolic of a general struggle, as the ESN(S) school had no physiotherapy help at the time of the interviews with the parents. However, eight parents had received some form of physiotherapy for their child (privately; from hospital; from previous schools etc.) and all eight said that they had received good practical help and advice. Six of the eight parents whose child had received physiotherapy thought that their child could still benefit from physiotherapy if it was available, as did two others whose children had never had regular physiotherapy:

M   "One more thing, they could do with a physiotherapist at school couldn't they?

GM   Yes, that school needs a physiotherapist badly. They can't get one because they don't pay enough money for them anyway. (....) But X is at school all day getting nothing. (....) The teachers have got quite enough to do without physiotherapy."

Two parents had stopped taking their child privately for physiotherapy, and two more had stopped because their child could now walk. Three parents had had to give up physiotherapy provision for their child because of the inconvenience of a hospital-based service. This inconvenience consists of difficulties with transport and the need for the child to have time off school to go to the hospital appointments. In practice a beneficial service becomes unavailable. One other child in this sample had stopped having physiotherapy since the parents had moved to the town from another area.

Even when a service is available by virtue of being statutory - as is the case with schooling - it may be that the most useful aspect of the service is informal and not so readily available. Six parents had favourable opinions about the teachers at the ESN(S) school, seemingly because most were women who were prepared to offer the mothers informal support. This support included taking the children on holiday; looking after a child for a weekend; making a fuss of the child's brother or sister when the mother was up at the school, and so on. Other favourable evaluations of the teachers, again expressed by six of the parents, included appreciation of the work, progress and stimulation that the school offered the child. In addition, three parents mentioned the low teacher-pupil ratio in the special school, and two mothers appreciated the special school for the relief from child-care that it afforded them during the day. However, perhaps most significant of all in relation to special (segregated) schooling, is that five parents mentioned the value to their children of the occasional contact with ordinary so-called 'normal' children. Ironically the aspect of the service that is found so helpful is the very aspect which goes against the whole initial orientation of the service (i.e. segregated schooling).

M   "But that's one thing the (head-teacher) is doing at (ESN(S) school). Our children go out to other schools for the day. And they have other children from normal schools come into their schools. So they're trying to integrate them, so that other kids understand."

The problems surrounding voluntary services and groups seem not so much that they do not exist, but that there are a variety of intervening factors which prevent parents deriving maximum benefit from such groups. In this sample of twenty children, eight parents made no mention of voluntary societies. Six parents mentioned voluntary societies dealing with specific handicaps (e.g. Down's Association) and all but one of these claimed to be fairly active in the society. Eight parents were members of the more generic MENCAP, though of these only two claimed to be active.

F   "Well, we're members (of MENCAP) because we pay our money, but we don't attend it (...)

M   A lot of it is mentally-handicapped adults as opposed to the young children. But that's our fault because they keep trying to get new people, you know, younger parents to go on the committees, but you've only got so much time and we tend to devote ours to the school."

This observation becomes especially pertinent when we go on to consider various ways in which parents' time and energy is wasted by certain services.

(e) <u>Professional Routines</u>
Most of the children were seen by paediatricians somewhere between once a month and once every three

months in the early stages, falling away to between once every six months and once every two years as the child grew older. The various routines which are part of having to go and see these doctors were heavily criticized. Over half the parents complained of the time spent waiting or the system of appointments by which several parents are given the same appointment time.

> M   "It worries me if you're waiting/You see when I'm on my own and I've got X up there for an appointment and I've got to be back by 12 o'clock for (X's brother) from the school. Because you usually have quite a wait really when we go up there. Usually up there for, well, hour and a half, sometimes two hours. But it's all according to how they are with their appointments, you know."

Several mentioned the variety of understudies they saw at different appointments, rather than seeing the senior consultant paediatrician.

> M   "(Senior consultant paediatrician) himself put him on this diet about four or five months ago, and I've never seen him once since I've been up the hospital. It's always been someone else I've seen. So I've never really seen (senior consultant) to sit down and say well this diet's not helping him. You know, shall I take him off? Shall I carry on with him or what? You know, I've never really sat down and talked about it."

A few were worried that the doctors would not criticize other professionals in order to get at what was best for the child because they were more concerned with maintaining 'good' relationships with fellow professionals.

> M   "Well (paediatrician) came round, and it hadn't been wrote on. He'd asked for this chart to be done. I mean he's as much to blame because he wasn't firm enough with (the nurses). He'd asked for this

> chart to be done - behaviour chart - so he could note all fits down and everything. And .... he came in and there wasn't anything wrote on it. So he looked at me and he said, well you're here most of the day, he said, would you write on it?"

However, even official procedures are not adhered to if this does not suit the routines of the professionals. In the area studied the Community Health Service medical officers are part of the official procedure for referring children to special schools. However, in this study, three parents claimed never to have been seen by a medical officer, and eight parents thought their child had not been seen by a medical officer before starting special school.

(f)   Parents' Time Taken Up

From interviews with the parents it became clear that contact with professional services had to serve a useful purpose for parents and child if such contact was not to become a net drain on the time and energy resources of the parents. As far as practical help or advice was concerned, a quarter of the parents thought that the GP had little or nothing to offer. In the two cases where specific help was received this consisted in being referred to another person or service for help. By way of contrast three parents were appreciative of the practical advice that the health visitor had been able to give them.

> M   "I was lucky I had a good health visitor that came at birth when I first had X. And she advised me on all the things that I would need or that I could get."

Half the parents suggested that the doctors were efficient in dealing with special physical medical problems, but that otherwise they had little in the way of advice or practical help to offer:

> F   "The trouble is, I think we've found as X/ When she was born she fitted into a category because she was, she had this heart murmur and we/she had trouble with (specific medical condition), so she

> fitted into a, you know. (Paediatrician),
> he'd got something he could work on and
> he had her in every few weeks and
> listened to her heart and that, but then
> once that cleared up .... he hadn't
> got anything medically wrong with her.
> Cause she's perfectly healthy. She's as
> healthy as the other two are. She doesn't
> fit into any category and this is where
> the more skilled professional people you
> meet the less they can do for you." (my
> emphasis)

However, it was not only paediatricians who were sometimes felt to be taking up parents' time. The professionals claim that one of the main reasons for the two-week assessment of a child at the assessment unit, involving a large number of different professionals, is to get to the root of any problems. But for most of the parents this continued to be the main problem in their view, even after the child had been assessed:

> M   "You see our problem's been not really
>   knowing what X .....
> F   What category he came into (....) So er,
>   you know we still haven't got down to
>   the .... his problems.
> M   His main problems."

And whilst the aim of any assessment might be to cover all possibilities by comprehensive coverage, in fact a number of parents felt that the assessment had left out an important aspect (such as an EEG test).

(g) Insensitive Attitudes

Four of the parents mentioned a negative attitude on the part of their GP, who of course may well have been made to feel insecure through his/her lack of knowledge. On the other hand, three parents said that their GPs paid them special attention or had a generally positive and helpful attitude. Many of the parents implied that hospital doctors (though this was not usually the paediatricians) lacked humanity or basic sensitivities in dealing with the parents, as will be discussed in Chapter 5, p. 135 . A few parents mentioned antagonisms with the nurses they encountered, particularly when the mother was staying in hospital with the child.

> M "I went up to this first-year student and I said, um - I could see goose pimples all over him - I said, can I have a blanket for X's cot please, he's cold? So she looked at me and said, we don't put blankets on cots. So I said, well X is cold. So she said, well X shouldn't be asleep now should he? So I said, X is ill you know and if he needs to sleep then he sleeps. 'It's not you who's got to be with him at night if he doesn't sleep at night is it?' So I said, it's not you either is it, you're day staff. You know. I had a right barney with her."

And in two cases this friction with the parents was also characterized by the nurses being obstructive or lying. Another unhelpful response that the nurses had to the situation was to instruct the parents on the morals of their circumstances. Part of the reason why hospital nurses may be the subject of so much criticism for being insensitive may be that they are acting under orders from doctors, administrators or the nursing hierarchy, and that they have to conform to certain ward routines. This may be why, in contrast, four parents appreciated the visits of the specialized community nurse from the assessment hospital.

It will be discussed presently how half the parents had had some thoughts about possible schooling for their children other than the ESN(S) school. As far as the ESN(S) school itself was concerned, parents generally liked it for its open and family-like atmosphere, though two parents thought that this also meant that education was sometimes taken less than seriously. On the other hand, four parents did have some criticisms to make about the insensitive approach of some of the staff.

> M "Even at school, now, we do get it: he's spoilt and that. They don't understand. And this is some of the staff."

(h) Lack of Specific Knowledge

In view of some of the points made about GPs, it is perhaps not surprising that four parents in this sample said that they felt GPs lacked knowledge about handicaps. And related to this, five parents saw the support given by the paediatricians at the general hospital as the main source of medical help.

Health visitors too were felt not to have much knowledge about specific disabled conditions.

> M "The health visitors in (town) where I lived when I had X were bloody hopeless. They were. They couldn't tell me anything."

What effect specialist health visitors for the handicapped will have remains to be seen.

Only six of the parents from this sample of twenty mentioned or talked about hospital nurses during interview, and five of these six pointed to the nurses' lack of specific knowledge about handicap:

> M "The next morning the nurses came in to see me and they were all very kind, but there was none of them really who .... could help me. None of them had a handicapped son or daughter."

(i) Underestimation of the Child

The content of what doctors say to parents is the subject of many of their complaints. Many parents criticized the doctors, arguing that their child had been unfairly labelled or limited by the doctors. 'Once and for all' statements that are later proved to be incorrect are disliked as much as information that is kept back. Several parents felt that their child was underestimated by the doctors at the general hospital, because after a long wait the child was not at its best in the clinic, or reacted strongly against hospitals in general.

> M "You see the little boy who walked across this room right now wanting to turn (the tape recorder) on and off. (Paediatrician) has never seen that. All he's ever seen is

a little boy who's got his head on his mother's shoulder and cries all the time."

Furthermore, parents felt that their child was not at its best during the unit assessment by virtue of the stay in hospital that this involved. This suggests that hospital was not conducive to assessments and that it could easily set the child's progress back for it to be admitted into hospital for assessment:

M   "Wherever he goes I have to stay with him. And they try to pack as much in (....) because he frets so much. Well, what he actually does is withdraws whenever he goes into a hospital situation."

Just as parents felt the child was not at its best in clinics or assessment hospital, seven parents felt that the medical officer's test procedures, attitudes, or the general circumstances of the meeting meant that the child did not do itself justice in terms of achievement.

(j)   Services Found Inappropriate
At this point it would be as well to describe in some detail the institution that has been referred to as the "assessment hospital/unit". This hospital seems to combine several functions. It provides some long-stay residential care for the subnormal. It also provides some 'phased-care' intended to provide parents with some relief from the hard work of looking after their severely mentally-handicapped child by admitting the child to hospital at regular periods throughout the year, or sometimes for a specific period in an emergency. Other studies refer to this arrangement as 'shared-care' or 'respite-care'. The hospital also incorporates a multi-disciplinary child development assessment unit, a community nursing service, and various outpatient consultations, especially for young mentally-handicapped adults who have 'outgrown' paediatric involvement. Philp and Duckworth (1982) have commented on similar schemes.

" ... the high proportion of care provided in the apparently inappropriate long-term subnormality

> hospitals also reduces demand. Probably parents
> are reluctant to commit their children to an
> environment which they feel to be unlikely to
> match standards of care that they provide."
> (Philp and Duckworth, 1982, p.76)

In this group of twenty children over half had been
assessed in the child development unit at the hospital.
Others had been seen as outpatients by a doctor at the
hospital. Five had received short-term 'phased-care'
though not necessarily at the hospital itself. Only one set
of parents even suggested the possibility of long-term
placement at the hospital for their child. Nearly half of
the parents felt that short-term care was inappropriate
and would cause stress for the child or themselves. This
included three parents who were actually using the
phased-care arrangement. The remainder did not have any
formal arrangements for short-term care; even where this
meant having to forgo holidays. In fact when asked in the
interview whether their children had ever had short-term
care, three parents were embarrassed and offended by the
very question. On the other hand, two parents expressed
appreciation of the phased-care their child received at the
hospital. With regard to the assessment unit, six parents
felt that this did not tell them, or was not likely to tell
them, anything about their child that they did not already
know. In only one case did the parents mention any
definite benefit from the assessment. The type of
short-term care thought to be available affected the
degree to which parents found it acceptable and would be
prepared to make use of it. Moving from the most disliked
and least acceptable to the more popular we have,
respectively, large hospitals, community hospitals,
small-scale hospitals, small-scale local hostels, family
bungalows and temporary foster-parents:

> M   "I wouldn't put her in (assessment
>   hospital). It's too big. I wouldn't feel that
>   she was being looked after properly."
>
> F   "We can send him to (community hospital)
>   for a few days. But it breaks the routine.
>   And it will probably take him several
>   days to get back into a type of routine
>   (....) But (if) you throw him out (of his

routine). And, you know, he could be sleeping during the day and awake all night. And just won't eat."

M   "It would be nice to have a short-term care-centre here in (town). That would be nice."

M   "It's a proper little bungalow. And it's for handicapped people (in another county area). (The child) goes from school to the bungalow and sleeps there (....). But that is the sort of thing you want isn't it?"

M   "What they need is another set of parents (.....) Like this fostering idea, some counties have started it haven't they?"

Parents also found certain types of contact with the social workers inappropriate. Some parents seemed confused about what the role of the social workers actually was. Three parents, for example, said they were unsure precisely how a social worker could help them. Other parents thought that any contact with social workers meant that they were then a 'problem family' and was in itself an indicator of shame and moral unworthiness.

F   "I don't know what good they can do.
M   No, I think/They came/I think a social worker came when I first found out about X, but they didn't feel there was a need to come back - but I think they're more if you have got social problems aren't they?"

(k)   Lack of Alternatives
The problems for parents do not even end with advice successfully given, received and understood, for the suggestions made by professionals may not work, particularly, as we have seen, if they are proposed specialist solutions to what are essentially ordinary problems. And so, for example, we find that parents complained that no alternatives or second line suggestions were mentioned by doctors.

Since the medical officer is evidently an important line to the ESN(S) school, it is worth noting that half the parents either wanted or had considered other types of schooling for their child. This included ESN(Moderate) school; school for the hearing-impaired; school for the physically-disabled; a special autism unit, and teaching by parents or tutor at home:

M   "Rex Brinkworth who runs the Down's Children's Association (....) he assessed her and said: all right, perhaps she's not the most brainy of the children but she should be in an 'M' school not an 'S'. She needs pushing and her speech won't come on with children that don't speak, she's got to be with children who do speak."

F   "Because it's been suggested also that if he's proved to be deaf well then this school could be the wrong school for him anyway."

M   " ... he might possibly get moved to another school .... you know in the future, to (school for the physically disabled) which is like for physically-handicapped more than mentally-handicapped."

M   "At the moment all the children (....) they've got various handicaps at X's school. I'd like to see more sort of specialized units for autistic children.

M   "They thought I was doing better for X at home than going to (the old ESN(S) school)."

However, several parents implied that the special ESN(S) school had been presented as the natural or logical place that their child should go. Indeed as an outside observer I had the impression that the professionals played on the relief of many parents that any form of education for their children existed to render special school placement uncontroversial.

M   "I think really she was two before we realized that she'd ...... um ...... she'd have to go to a special school. It wasn't until (Medical officer) came to see us and he sort of put us straight with it all."

As with the medical officer, four parents felt that the educational psychologist had been involved in persuading them to let their child go to a special school, as if there were no alternatives.

From this section it seems that in addition to practical problems, the parents of mentally-handicapped children also have various difficulties dealing with the services. Resources that could be used to help are often not. And so parents are sometimes not listened to by the professionals; they are not given information; the therapy services that are found so useful are the ones least available, and parents are dependent on the discretion of professionals to refer them to other services. Then, two of the parents' most important resources for dealing with problems - time and energy - are continually frustrated. Parents' time is taken up by professional routines without necessarily having anything to show for it, and there is the continual emotional worry of how they and the child are going to be treated. Finally, there is little scope for the parents to actively shape the services. They have to deal with people who may lack knowledge about handicaps, or who underestimate the child; whose services are not always found helpful, whilst at the same time there seem to be no alternatives.

FILES AND MEETINGS

This section deals with the way that the services for mentally-handicapped children are dealt with by the professionals in their meetings and files.

(a) Professional Knowledge

Although it is the contention of this study that there are important similarities between medical, psychological and other types of professional knowledge, in the following arguments the examples are nearly all medical. This reflects firstly, that many services for mentally-handicapped children are from doctors or professionals based in hospitals, and secondly, the method of the study which, in looking for formal contact between parents and professionals as a source of data, reflects the large proportion of files and meetings which have a medical setting.

Medical knowledge of mentally-handicapped children, developed by looking at such children as special categories, can be useful when such knowledge is technical, dealing with physical impairment and concentrating on the child when very young. Both the parents and the paediatrician may then feel that later clinics are routine and their content generally trivial. A doctor may implicitly recognize this orientation of medical knowledge to technicalities at a young age, but the parents continue to be frustrated by being recalled for routine clinics. The doctor might be fearing a deterioration in the child's condition, or accusations of negligence if he does not continue to monitor the child. But perhaps because the doctor's thinking is trapped in strictly medical terms, he forgets that by not letting go he reduces the possibility for other types of help. For example, the scarce time of the parents might more beneficially be spent on therapy as the child grows older and leaves behind certain physical medical problems. But the doctors may be so concerned with identifying the boundary of medicine, that they fail to recognize the useful work that therapists do:

> "I have arranged for her to have some physiotherapy, mainly to give the mother an additional source of support." - Files: Doctor.

An important part of professional knowledge is the keeping of records which can be referred to as 'facts' (to develop Stimson and Webb, 1975, p. 54). This is one reason behind the various assessments and testings of the child, both at home and in hospital. The general feeling of parents (and indeed of some professionals who are not based in hospitals) is that children react badly to being in hospital and do not perform at their best in any assessment. The visit of a clinical medical officer to the home to test the child is another occasion when parents feel that it is expecting too much to think that a child will perform on demand and under time limit for a stranger. And after all, this is not an unreasonable view.

The doctor himself partly recognizes this:

> M "The trouble with him, if he's not in the mood ...
>
> DR He won't do it.
>
> M He won't do it. It's very frustrating 'cause you see/
>
> DR You know what he's capable of.
>
> M Absolutely and he ....
>
> DR .... And when somebody else comes to try and measure him (laughs)
>
> M Forget it." - Visit by medical officer.

But because he is vastly experienced in testing and assessing children the doctor will have heard such views many times before, and he therefore expects parents to overestimate the abilities of the child and to make excuses for it:

> F "You've caught him when he's really weary. Yes. You know.
>
> DR Yes, sure. I'm always doing this to youngsters.
>
> F Yes, well, yes.
>
> DR And all/Well I say, well, all right. All we can do is see what he does today.
>
> F That's right. Fair comment, yes.
>
> DR You know. And try and catch him at a different time another." - Visit by medical officer.

No doubt the doctor sees the stress of testing as a counterbalance to the claims of the parents. He may also feel that part of his role is to show parents why their claims are wrong or misguided. It is distressing to see some sociologists implicitly reflect the political outlook of the doctors, in particular the assumption that doctors are objective, neutral observers and therefore more likely to be right, and that parents are biased observers and therefore more likely to be wrong.

> "Thus parents would typically 'claim' their children were progressing, that they could do things at home that they 'wouldn't' do in the clinic (.....) children's limitations, often demonstrated

by the doctor, served to show the parents that
his typification of the child was correct." (Davis,
A., 1982, p. 124)

The doctor might claim that the conditions are the same
for all children, but it would be a misleading claim.
Children who are not handicapped are not usually subject
to such close observation and detailed testing. Neither the
doctor nor Davis reflects sufficiently on what happens
with so-called 'normal' children, which leaves the parents'
views of how a normal child would react with strong
claims:

M   "Well, (doctor) has this case and he
comes in with it. Well, it's obvious that a
child is intrigued by what he's got in his
case, you know. I mean any child,
whether it be subnormal or normal. And
all X was interested in was what he had
got in his case. But he opens it a little
bit and takes what he wants out and then
shuts it, you see. Well, X wasn't
interested in what he'd got out. He was
only interested in what was left in the
box, in the case. And I know for a fact
our little girl would be just the same and
she's perfectly normal." - Parental
interview.

In fact this points to the unstated political bias of Davis,
for he actually has examples from Local Authority Child
Welfare Clinics with which to make comparisons. Children
considered 'normal' from commonsense observation are
excused failure at certain tests.

" ... 'failure' was remedied by checking with the
mother that the child could normally do it and
the 'failure' explained away as due to character,
setting or temperament." (Davis, A., 1982, p. 55)

The inappropriate views that doctors and other
professionals hold over testing and hospital assessments
stem from professional knowledge that, by specializing in
looking at one group, do not consider the rest of the
population. Although agreeing with parents that tests and

assessments are inappropriate in that the child reacts against the situation and performs badly, the main point is not so much that the mentally-handicapped are underestimated by professionals, but that the stupidity of the rest of the population is underestimated. Looking at the other end of the spectrum it might be argued that it is the knowledge and intelligence of professionals and academics that is popularly overestimated, and that this misconception is deliberately or inadvertently perpetuated by them. Perhaps this is what is happening when doctors make references to themselves as representatives of medical knowledge in general. One conclusion is not that the mentally-handicapped are necessarily more clever than generally thought, but that the rest of us are that much more stupid.

But it is not just misleading tests and inappropriate stays in hospital which result from compiling records as the 'facts' of professional knowledge. Compiling records on categories of children seen as special and separate leads to considering and recording the available services as 'facts' to refer to. Thus placement of a child in a special school comes to be regarded by some doctors not as a particular political option but as a further indication that the child is abnormal. It is not an attempt to help educate the children but a sad consequence of being handicapped and even an institutional confirmation of that handicap.

> "Will need to attend (special school) if he lives until 5 years." - Files: Doctor

The very real danger of such misplaced attitudes is more than the mere fact of contact with certain services being seen as an indication that the child is indeed handicapped. It is that by perversely seeing contact with a service (which may not be able to offer help) just as a confirmation of handicap, that doctors may come to assume that because they cannot offer any help, nobody can. This again is part of the unwillingness of doctors to give up their jurisdiction to other people who can help the severely handicapped such as therapists and parents themselves.

(b) Limits to Professional Knowledge

There is little doubt that the professionals, especially the doctors, suffer anxieties about their lack of knowledge. Amongst other things they may mistakenly feel that they are being ridiculed when the fact of their lack of knowledge is clearly seen by parents.

> DR "..... and then (doctors) sort of say, well we don't know much about him.
>
> M Well, no. They have to read his case history first which takes about an hour.
>
> F Yes.
>
> M And then they ask me what/what I want (laughs)
>
> F What medicine.
>
> DR Yes.
>
> M 'What shall we give him?' (laughs)" - Visit by medical officer.

If it is true that doctors dealing with what is usually called mental handicap sometimes do not know what to do to help, then they may come to rely exclusively on the limited types of help they can offer. This may involve monitoring the child's progress through routine clinics, assessment in hospital, developmental testing, or crisis help by admission to hospital. This is not to say, however, that with specific types of hospital (a smaller, local community hospital where the parents and child are informally known) or under specific conditions (an assessment hospital for a limited time and a specific purpose) that some hospital provision is not helpful for parents. However, there is some evidence from the meetings between professionals and parents that professionals who are not based in hospitals recognize, to a degree, the inappropriate nature of certain hospital provision.

> F "Do you think it's worth er X going to have/get some assessment? Your personal feeling?
>
> DR I, I/I think it depends on what you are looking for with assessment. Now you have got a very definite thing. You are concerned about this slapping and .... things. And the way he responds.

F	He gets frustrated.
DR	He gets frustrated.
F	And we can't/
DR	And you can't find what it is that frustrates him.
F	Right, that's right.
DR	Well it could well be that they can ..... find an answer.
F	That's a good idea.
DR	But in other respects you see, I sometimes think, well ...... you're going along there. You will see ..... a psychologist. Well we've got ..... you know, educational psychologists within the authority who are seeing the children in schools. You see a speech therapist there. We already have speech therapists. So ....
F	Right.
DR	In some respects I do wonder ..... how much you do .... get. (.....)
DR	There is good co-operation. But it's just that I wonder sometimes ......
F	Mmn.
DR	What you are .....
M	Hoping for.
(F	Yes.
(DR	Hoping for." - Visit by medical officer.

It is precisely this ambivalence which leaves parents in an awkward situation where they feel they cannot criticize the services as something has ostensibly been done (the child has been assessed in hospital) but yet sense that nothing substantive has been achieved or is likely to be achieved. It is this type of situation which will deter parents from telling the doctors concerned exactly what they feel about the service, or which will mean that when they do criticize a service, it is not directed to the professional concerned:

M	"But I still keep in with the hospital because you've got to. You've got to keep in with the hospital because you don't know when you're going to need them for anything really." - Parental interview.

It may be that parents will sometimes offer criticism to another professional who is not directly involved, perhaps in the hope that their criticism will be passed on. But the professionals are unlikely to do this because they want relations between themselves and other professionals to be as friendly and smooth-running as possible. However, it also seems that the professionals cannot conceive of themselves asking the parents whether or not they wish their criticisms to be passed on. If, then, we have a situation where the limits to professional knowledge mean that the doctors and other professionals have little to offer in certain instances, and are also uncertain what is expected of them (because parents are fearful to voice their criticisms directly or openly) then this can only mean the continuation of professional routines which are of doubtful value to the parents and child. Quite apart from representing what little the professionals can do, some clinics or meetings may be initiated because the professional may feel they are part of a bureaucratic duty or fears complaint if they are not undertaken. In one instance an educational psychologist is aware that he has put a mother to a lot of trouble to meet him at the special school, but this awareness is not acted upon and the mother is required to make her way to the school for the meeting anyway. Similarly, a time-consuming recall to the paediatric clinic may concern a paediatrician if he is sensitive to the difficulties of a mother who is facing a service which is now less than appropriate. But again, monitoring may be all the doctors can offer, and this perception is likely to be strengthened by the knowledge that the emphasis of their legal responsibilities is on 'being there' rather than being relevant or even clinically accurate, to judge by the outlook of the Medical Defence Union:

> "Even inadequate treatment or mistaken diagnosis are not a breach unless the doctor failed .... to make a reasonable clinical decision. Thus a doctor who mistakes a perforated appendix for gastroenteritis with a fatal result was found .... not to be in breach of his terms of service because he had visited the patient when requested and had made careful examinations

which he had meticulously recorded in his notes."
- Medical Defence Union Annual Report (quoted
in The Guardian)

As has already been argued, a consequence of doctors
clinging to inappropriate or irrelevant sources of contact
creates inappropriate professional routines which make it
difficult for such useful services as therapy to be given. In
this example, a physiotherapist has to break the rules in
order to provide a much-needed service - a basic human
right of enabling a disabled child to lie in a comfortable
manner.

> HT   "We haven't got the skills to make him
> comfortable. Although it did help very
> much when (physiotherapist) came across.
>
> T   Very much. And she didn't really come to
> see X. She was only allowed to come and
> see (a different child), who she has in
> (assessment hospital).
>
> HT   Mmn.
>
> T   I asked her. I said, would you please look
> at X? Which she did, but she said bring
> the children there if I want ..../" -
> Educational case-conference.

When professionals are faced with the limitations of
their knowledge and are uncertain what to do, a further
way to do what they can is to make a record of the
problem. This is one reason for comments in the files
which refer to an additional benefit of a service which
supposedly exists in the first instance for totally different
reasons.

> "I have not seen the boy myself but would
> support Dr. A's recommendation that he be
> admitted to the special care unit attached to
> (ESN(S) school), the length of attendance per
> week to be negotiated between the unit and the
> parents - the aim being largely parental relief." -
> Files: Educational Psychologist.

The doctors and psychologists are uncertain what their
knowledge has to offer, and all they feel they can do is to
implicitly record the burden of work from which the

mother requires regular rest and thus show that they recognize the problem. But once again the fatalism of the comment stems from their own inability to help, and denies the very real possibility that teachers and therapists can offer the child good practical help.

It is this inability/unwillingness to see the problems in terms other than the limits to the profession's own knowledge that leads doctors (and unfortunately some parents who accept the doctor's view) to perceive a crisis for medicine. The richly-financed high technology procedures of medicine can save increasing numbers of severely mentally-handicapped, so the argument goes, but for what, since medicine then comes up against its own inability to help.

> "In the past year the child has been severely ill on two occasions. On both occasions we gave him only nursing care, expecting that these episodes were terminal." - Files: Doctor

> "Any more interference would only stop further deterioration and prolong the child's unhappy life." - Files: Doctor

The problem has several dimensions. Firstly, the view that professionals have of the world is based on the general exclusion of the mentally-handicapped from their educational and social lives, which reinforces the second point, namely that their professional knowledge is constructed from a situation where the mentally-handicapped are socially segregated and considered as a distinct category of person. Thirdly, sympathy for those who face long-term care in hospital or survive through high technology medical treatment is based on the view that the reality of the services available is the only possible reality. This last point is reinforced by the political conservatism of professionals which is an understandable reaction to a society where jobs are not a basic human right but an outcome of competition between different people. It is doubtful, for example, that sympathetic recognition of the necessarily inadequate long-term care in hospital would be matched by a willingness to see a massive transfer of resources to the community, if this meant hospital staff losing their jobs. The consequences of this misconceived crisis for medicine is that the doctors impose this crisis on the parents - parents, it is supposed, must surely react in certain ways. Far from helping parents and child towards a so-called 'normality' the comments by the doctors in their files indicate the ways they inadvertently contribute to stigmatizing the parents. One way is to treat the reactions of parents as pathologies that need to be overcome. Thus parents tend to be seen as either 'overprotective' or as not having 'accepted' their child's handicap. Related to this is the way in which popular stereotypes are confirmed. Being in contact with Social Services or being a single parent are both taken as indices of inadequacy. Furthermore the distinction between deserving and undeserving recipients of state benefits is reproduced in the files of the professionals. By doing this they implicitly maintain the stigma which all recipients suffer.

> "The family are very self-reliant and they make
> light of their work as parents but I think a day
> attendance allowance would be justified and
> might be a help to them in the good care they
> provide." - Files: Assessment Unit.

It is not only the parents who are affected - just as doctors try to get parents to accept their view so the parents will follow their advice, so doctors may try to persuade other professionals to act as they, the doctor, see fit.

> "I would be grateful if the Social Services
> Department in (town) would look into the
> question of helping this family in their home and
> in their general needs as a handicapped family
> with a seriously handicapped child." - Files:
> Paediatrician.

A consequence of this is that any contact with certain services in itself involves a departure from 'normality', however successful the parents may be in treating the child (and getting others to treat the child) as 'normally' as possible, a strategy termed 'normalization' by F. Davis (1963). It is now possible to see how professionals' arrogance is built up, not as an attribute of an individual, but as a product of the various factors discussed. Here a social worker condescends to deliver a scarce and precious resource, namely his/herself.

> "We discussed quite fully her feelings about X and the effect X has on the family, and I felt the time I was able to give was well worthwhile." - Files: Social Worker.

The limits to professional knowledge mean that the content of professional discourse becomes the way in which parents relate to the service - the appropriateness of their reactions, their worthiness to receive the service etc. In such circumstances the various contacts with services (including researchers) all work against a normal existence for parents and child. In some senses, therefore, the distinctiveness of parents and mentally-handicapped children is self-fulfilling.

Not only does the issue for the professionals become: how have the parents reacted to the services? Because the limits to professional knowledge constitute the very reasons why services become distorted in the ways discussed above, it is in fact extremely likely that parents will not react as professionals hope or expect they would. For example, the obvious lack of knowledge that GPs have about disability, coupled with the expertise that the mothers have, will reduce the possibility of parents following the strategies suggested by the doctors.

> F   "The thing was, you see, by the time she had the fit (GP) said he knew we were going to see (paediatrician) today, which is .... like a fortnight. So he said he'd leave it till then he said.
> (....)
> F   Then the doctor did come. He wasn't quite sure. She seemed to come out of it but/the doctor couldn't tell.
> (....)
> F   Um .... she's had a lot of infections according to the ... the er .... doctors that she's seen." - Paediatric clinic.

Paediatricians as well are caught up in the technical emphasis of medicine and therefore the limitations of medical knowledge.

> "I have had a number of investigations done and none of them have shown any abnormality. I would be grateful for your help with the management of his handicap." - Files: Paediatrician.

And so long as other hospital doctors think in such technically specific terms, situations are bound to arise where operations are a possibility. The doctors may suspect that children who have been labelled 'mentally-handicapped' are not going to improve anyway, and from a sense of sympathy for the child may wish to spare it the pain and trouble of an operation which may have very little benefit for the child:

> "One wonders whether it is worthwhile treating this amblyopia enthusiastically in a child such as this." - Files: Surgeon.

But here the doctors have become so engrossed in making the decision that they appear to forget the powerful position they are in and forget to go through the routine of informing and consulting the parents. It may be that such consultations would always end in agreement. But not to inform parents appears not only as professional arrogance, but sets a dangerous precedent of not offering the parents an opportunity to consult. A further example is when doctors congratulate themselves on the virtues of a regular paediatric review, seemingly unaware of the frustration and irritation this form of arrangement causes the mother (fieldwork diary).

(c) Expectations that Professionals have of Parents
There is considerable variation between parents as to how much responsibility they would like to take in making decisions affecting their child. Some seem to be very reliant on the opinions of doctors, for example:

> HV "So eventually we thought about the bed alarm which she's using at the moment. Er, (mother) went along to the GP and asked, you know, if it was OK to use it." - Educational Review.

Unfortunately this encourages the misconception that all

parents want professionals to make the decisions for them. At the same time this misconception helps confirm the view that doctors (and other professionals) have of themselves, namely that they are best able to judge a situation because they have the specialist knowledge. Certainly doctors are in powerful positions to make decisions affecting a child and its parents. The danger is that the social skill of the doctor in managing the relationship with the parent (based on the doctors' expectation that the parents want them to take the responsibility for decisions) becomes mistaken for the idea that the doctor has a distinctive knowledge which suggests to the doctor which practical help should be given.

The expectation that parents are happy to leave decision-making to the professionals is one of the reasons that certain activities of voluntary or parents' groups make the professionals very defensive and protective. This is particularly illustrated by a discussion on the Down's Association in an educational review - a discussion for which there are no direct quotations as I was instructed to turn the tape recorder off. The professionals (including teachers, doctors and psychologists) knew the controversial nature of what was being said, as they commented that I had missed recording the most interesting part of the review. Part of the discussion suggested that groups like the Down's Association should be 'ginger groups' to the educational system. Furthermore, it was said, they should strike a balance between being over-subdued, and being over-imposing (with the associated dangers of misleading parents or raising their anxieties) (fieldwork diary). One suspects that professionals regard such groups as a threat in various ways. Firstly, they give parents more confidence, which would suggest that this would lead to increasing numbers asserting their right to be involved in decision-making. The professionals may see this almost as a corruption of the parents' usual deference, without seeing that their power and the parents' lack of information (not to mention simple habit of the way things are) can equally be viewed as a corruption of their assertiveness. Secondly, parents' groups represent a threat as an alternative source of knowledge. Indeed, professionals may be worried that parents will discover how little they know. This is because the professionals think they should be independent, not subject to outside control from administration or voluntary groups, accountable mainly to members of their own profession, all with the aim of maintaining a personal control over their working conditions (Cartwright and Anderson, 1981, p. 75). No doubt they see this control as a means to increased knowledge. Unfortunately this means that possibly the greatest potential source of knowledge - the parents - is denied, and makes the professionals seem arrogant to the extent they presume rigidly that they know what is best, even in the face of organized groups of parents.

It follows that if professionals continue to think that they know best, they will expect parents to follow the recommendations they make. This expectation probably also derives from how professionals achieve their self-esteem; their wish for professional independence and personal control over their working conditions, and their need to sense that their job is rewarding (thus a vocation, or a calling) - in fact much of what it means to be a professional. This is all particularly true of doctors, who try to get the parents to accept a medical perspective (Stimson and Webb, 1975, p. 81). And so it is that in the files are recorded the well-meant offers of help from various doctors and hospitals, seemingly unaware of how, or why, they are often inappropriate. For example, the following comment denies both the work that the mother does in being the mainstay of health-care for her child and her view that since GPs and health visitors know little about disabling conditions, the primary source of what little medicine has to offer is the paediatrician:

> "Help from the Primary Health Care Team i.e. the General Practitioner and the Health Visitor."
> - Files: Assessment Unit.

Thus a service may be offered with little awareness as to whether the mother may consider the service appropriate, nor as to the work and inconvenience that may be involved in liaising with that service. Indeed, it is only a professional from outside the local authority who seems able to criticize any of the local services as inappropriate in any particular case:

> "This improvement provides further evidence that it was the changes at (assessment hospital) which were largely responsible for the disturbed behaviour." - Files: Doctor.

The unfortunate consequence of all this arises when parents, quite reasonably, wish to disagree with professionals and do not wish to follow the course of action suggested. The fact of recording that parents have turned down the opportunity of using a service (however inappropriate the parents may have found that service or felt it to be) firstly protects the professionals, and secondly implicitly criticizes the parents. The negative impression of them is then left on file where it cannot be challenged.

> "Unfortunately the parents did not agree to this assessment and the case-conference, which was to have been held to discuss our assessment findings, was therefore cancelled." - Files: Medical Officer.

Associated with this feeling of professionals that parents do not want responsibility for decisions, is the expectation that parents may feel inhibited if it is left to them to contact services when they want. For example, doctors may expect that parents would find it difficult to ask a paediatrician to see their child again, after earlier saying that they felt they did not need the help and withdrawing from the service. In fact there is considerable disagreement among parents about whether they find routine clinics comforting or irritating, or feel ambivalent about them. But the recall of parents and child to the paediatric clinic is often treated as entirely logical and unquestioned. Again the consequences of such a view is that how and when parents and child are seen in the clinic is more determined by the doctors' own routines or simply habit than any apparent medical necessity:

> DR   "And then I'll see you in/How often do I see you? Six months?
> M   Six monthly, yes.
> DR   Seems about right." - Paediatric clinic.
>
> DR   "How often do you come? Once a year?"
>   - Paediatric clinic.

If it is true that parents would be reluctant to re-establish contact after a break, how much more difficult it must be to break through medical routines and tactfully suggest withdrawing from the service. The apparently simple solution of asking parents in each case how, when and if they wish their child to continue to be seen will not seem possible to the doctors so long as they also think they are expected to appear in control, and that being in control is part of what it means to be a good professional.

Being in control takes us back to the expectation of the professionals that parents want them to take on the responsibility of making decisions. This creates further problems if the strategy of the parents is to try and bring their child up in as much a so-called 'normal' way as possible. The parents may have to deal with offers from the professionals of services which in themselves work against attempts to treat the child 'normally'. As far as possible then, the parents will want to resolve issues surrounding the use of drugs, for example, to ensure that they clearly benefit the child, for if they do not their demoralizing effect constitutes an additional social handicap that both parents and child can well do without.

> M   "But they asked at (assessment hospital) about did I think the valium was doing any good cause they/(paediatrician) raised it a bit. But I said no, we don't feel that it is calming him down any. But has he still got to be on it that's what I wanted to ..../" - Paediatric clinic.

Furthermore, the parents may only want advice in order to make their decision about how best to carry on their strategy of treating their child as 'normally' as possible. This will mean a varied reaction to various different services offered. Sometimes this will result in a mother resisting using a service when it is clearly something that would not usually be a 'normal' part of family life.

> DR   "Does he ever have any sort of phased-care at (assessment hospital)?
> M   No. They have said that he could if I wanted him to. But my parents have him." - Paediatric clinic.

Conversely this means that some types of services which fit the child more into the 'normal' run of things are greeted enthusiastically by some parents. A good example of this is the partial integration of some of the children into local mainstream schools:

> HT "This term he's going out for an
> afternoon a week to the local playschool
> .... playgroup.
> (....)
>
> T (The children) didn't want to come back
> did they?
> (....)
>
> T The parents seem eager too." - Educational
> case-conference.

This will also mean that the view that the professionals
have of the world and their power to define what is
expected to happen to the child socially will be called into
question. Since the life experiences of a handicapped child
will be of a somewhat different nature from a so-called
'normal' child, certain professionals have often to be
reminded not to judge the child on more stringent criteria
than 'normal'.

> EP "The formal teaching is a very sort of
> stiff, formal thing. And that's not where
> he's most responsive and yet you can/
>
> T But he's only four yet isn't he?
>
> EP Yeh, right. You can't/
>
> T You think of a normal four year old
> (laughs) I mean. They don't go to school."
> - Meeting between Educational Psychologist
> and Teacher.

On the other hand if the criteria become too lax the
struggle for 'normality' is undermined for the parents in a
different way:

> M "(Teacher) said that his name had been
> brought up to go into that (assessment
> class). And she felt that/not to go in.
> And she wants to have him for another
> year. And apparently (head-teacher) said
> .... er in the first place that she
> wanted him to go in.
> (....)
>
> M It's lovely that they love him. And I think
> it's lovely/it's brilliant. But he's got to

	knuckle down and do it.
DR	Yes. Oh yes, it's .... you know that there is the danger that while he stops sort of in the special care units, the nursery units ... it's still a lot of play.
M	Yes, absolutely. I couldn't agree with you more." - Visit by medical officer.

And so, in a variety of ways, the expectations that professionals have make it difficult for them to be flexible, and make liaising with the services an increasingly fraught task for the parents.

(d) How the Relationship between Professionals and Parents is Managed

One of the ways in which doctors (and other professionals) feel they have to manage their relationships is that in being a scarce resource they need to protect themselves against abuse and exploitation (Stimson and Webb, 1975, p. 59). The politics of controlling the numbers entering medical school to create such a scarce resource are not dealt with here. One of the most important features of this protective practice is 'gatekeeping' (Stimson and Webb, 1975, p. 118), ensuring that parents have passed through the 'appropriate channels' and that no-one in the medical hierarchy has been offended. Here a registrar is concerned to see that the parents have passed through the appropriate 'gatekeepers'.

M	"Er we did have a little problem getting back into the (district authority) once we'd been to (specialist hospital).
DR	Mmn.
M	But I think that's all right now.
DR	Where had you been? Which authority? You left and/
M	Well we/Well .... X had an assessment at (assessment hospital). It was recommended that he went for this hearing test at (specialist hospital). He went in. So I took him. And of course/
DR	On your own, on your own?
M	Er, my doctor recommended it. That's my family doctor.

DR   Your doctor recommended it.
M   Well .... When X lost a hearing aid a few weeks ago.
DR   Mmn.
M   When I phoned up (local hospital)/
DR   Did (paediatrician) know this?
M   (Paediatrician) knew, yes.
DR   He knew?
M   Yes". - Paediatric clinic.

There are two points that need to be made here. One is that the doctor may become so involved in managing the professional-client relationship as he sees fit that the real problems of the mother and child become lost at the expense of such routine questioning. The other is that this concern may mean that the distribution of services will not be arranged in the best interests of the child or the parents. For example, a paediatrician may be worried about his own professional relationship with the parents' and child's GP. He may be aware that some GPs are unhappy about their relationship with consultants, with delays, inadequate communication, and relative lack of status as some of the causes of the trouble (Cartwright, 1967, p. 141). The paediatrician may then try to ensure that the parents respect the GP as a means of access to the paediatrician to restrict unreasonable demands on the consultant especially for problems that are perhaps considered to be the province of GPs.

DR   "I think if you're still unhappy about him, then your family doctor, who is it, Dr. A. isn't it?
M   Er, yes, I usually see B. actually.
DR   You see Dr. B. do you? OK. Well I'd get in touch with him if X is no better. He'd clearly be willing to help with his management." - Paediatric clinic.

But if, as in this case, the contact with the GP can involve long waits at the surgery to see a doctor who freely admits to knowing nothing about the associated medical problems of disabling conditions and often asks the parents what drugs he should prescribe, then the parents and child will have clearly lost out in the niceties of managing relationships. And yet how can parents be expected to explain their predicament to either of these doctors without offending people they may like because of the concern they show for the child? Similarly, a paediatrician may reasonably feel that everyone should have equal access to certain services. The paediatrician then feels obliged to prevent parents using a useful service they have found only because the usual channels had not been gone through.

> DR "What we're not wanting to do is to offer you something that we can't offer other children otherwise we can't be strictly fair or flexible.
>
> M Oh, I see, yes.
>
> DR Now (medical officer) does have access to facilities which children with X's sort of problems do have legitimate claim, OK?" - Paediatric clinic.

Once again, protective practices end up by being an obstacle to the spontaneous emergence of the types of services parents find most useful.

Other professionals as well may see themselves as a scarce resource open to abuse. This concern is based on the idea of professional independence and being the one who is qualified to judge what is best. Other resources that parents might draw on are seen as a threat, and there is an implicit condemnation of the parents.

> ST "Mum told me that a teacher goes in through the long summer holidays. I don't know about other holidays.
>
> HT Yes. Well, if that's happening we need to have a link up because we might be working at very different goals and different ways and it's going to confuse X." - Educational case-conference.

One of the concerns of the professionals when parents draw on other resources and thereby have access to alternative sources of information is that parents will have their hopes falsely raised. This is precisely the type of criticism made during the professionals' discussion of the Down's Association (see above, pp. 103-4   ). When professionals talk of people raising false hopes in parents

there seems no way of distinguishing whether the hopes
are in principle false because of the necessary
consequences of the child's condition, or whether they are
false in practice because the local services either cannot
or will not change to meet needs which in principle could
be met. In either case the professionals may well be
worried that parents will be led to question the nature of
the services provided. This worry seems to be behind the
professionals' comments on Rex Brinkworth of the Down's
Association who apparently organizes his own assessments
of Down's Syndrome children for parents. The form that
the protection of professionals seems to take here is for
them to attack his personal credibility. Thus it was argued
that he raised false hopes in other parents of Down's
children. Questions were raised about what medical or
psychological qualifications he had, and whether he really
understood what certain types of developmental scales
meant. It was said that he continually over-stepped his
jurisdiction in his activities, and that he generalized too
much from his own Down's daughter who was exceptional
for that syndrome. He was also 'mischievous' if he was
attempting to reduce the principles of school placement to
developmental scores (fieldwork diary). This conversation
highlights another fear of the professionals which they
seem to have to manage in professional-client relationships,
namely that other resources and information increases the
ability of the parents to judge the services they are
offered (Stimson and Webb, 1975, p. 134). For example,
the professionals would not want the criteria of admission
to special school to become established and known because
then they can be held accountable by their own
procedures. Thus in establishing their attack on the
Down's Association, the professionals argued that children
with 'General Quotients' (based on the same principles as
Intelligence Quotients) between 50 and 60 would usually be
under consideration for a place in ESN(M) education, but
not if they were Down's children because the ESN(M)
school had not yet got the 'language-based curriculum' to
cope. This contradicts the very criterion that a
psychologist uses to persuade another mother to allow her
child to be sent to the ESN(M) school:

> EP   "There they'll be concentrating on things
>   like reading and writing that/They've not
>   pushed that sort of thing here at (ESN(S)

school) because there are more important things to do for most of the kids." - Meeting between Educational Psychologist and Mother.

The professionals also adopt protective practices as a result of managing criticism or the possibility of criticism by the parents. Sometimes doctors may see criticism in the context of parents increasingly demanding their rights to certain services (Cartwright, 1967, p. 57), and their reaction may be to be as little involved as possible.

"Mrs. X telephoned me last week complaining of a number of things (....) for my own part I am happy to fade into the background." - Files: Medical officer.

Doctors may also decide not to become involved if they fear that they will lose their professional independence and control over their working conditions.

"I think that at this stage it would be unwise to resume our involvement with the family as I suggest we would get dragged into the question of his school placement which should obviously be left to yourself and (other medical officer)." - Files: Medical officer writing to Educational psychologist.

But there is a problem with such concerns to see that the parents learn to abide by the various protective demarcations that doctors establish for themselves. And the problem is that the niceties of relationships come to be put above the best interests of the parents and child:

"The question of X's further referral either to (specialist hospital) or to the (specialist centre) is obviously a somewhat delicate one as (local specialist) has already indicated that he did not feel that (specialist hospital) could help (....) I think that this then would prove not to be too embarrassing to the parents and other professionals in their relationship with (local specialist)." Files: Medical officer.

Such problems are more complicated because professionals may come to feel through experience that having to explain a situation is very nearly the same thing as having to justify their actions (to develop Stimson and Webb, 1975, pp. 123-7). It is surely not unreasonable to expect professionals to be able to justify their procedures to the parents and children. In any case, often actions will not seem reasonable if they are not explained. If, in fearing complaints, professionals use files as an aggressive form of protection against accusations of incompetence, then their contents will often come to read as an attack on the parents, however 'neutral' the language the professional may feel has been used:

> "I listened to the parents' grumbles about the lack of contact from the various authorities but was able to remind them of my own letters to them of September 1978 and January of this year offering to see the parents when and where they chose." - Files: Doctor.

There is some evidence to suggest that professionals are often uncertain what is expected of them by parents. Some doctors, for example, make much out of the fact that parents are unlikely to have told them everything in a given situation (to develop Stimson and Webb, 1975, pp. 43-4). Indeed, whilst doing some preparatory work for the study, one paediatrician surprised me by asking after one clinic whether or not I felt that the mother had been telling the truth (fieldwork diary). Whilst acknowledging that this issue may seem a problem to the doctors, any response which presumes this of parents not only makes the doctors arrogant, but will also be self-fulfilling. That is, it will encourage the very secretiveness in parents that professionals claim they do not want, even though the very notion of professionalism arrogantly claims this secretiveness as a right of its own. Furthermore, this presumption that parents have not told them everything becomes one way in which professional stereotypes can be imposed on families. Here a doctor is trying to dissuade the parents from relying on a community hospital (a service they feel at ease with and find useful) and persuade them to use the assessment hospital (which some other parents cannot bring themselves to use at all and others only with great reluctance). The suggestion is that the family will slip further and further towards being a 'handicapped family' unless they make use of the services as suggested:

M   "Well, what I like is ..... I was finding very helpful with (community hospital) was just to be able to ring up when I was desperate and say, oh, can you have him for a couple of nights? (....)

DR   Now/certainly a lot of parents from children at (ESN(S) school) do find it helpful if they do have a regular break.

M   Yes.

DR   What we would call phased-care.

M   Yes.

DR   That you would make a/what should we say, a contract or an agreement with .... per/a hospital/probably (assessment hospital).

F   Yes.

DR   To/Whereby they would say to you let us try and arrange a break - might be a week every six months. It might be a week every three months.

M   Oh, I see, yes.

DR   Just on a regular basis, so that it gives you something to look forward to. The fact that you will have a period without .... er X. And er/and during that week, you know, you can give all your time probably to (sister).

M   Yes. Oh, yes.

DR   Because she does I am sure/Does she ever comment about what she can't do?" - Visit by medical officer.

Once again it is the task of persuasion in itself that comes to constitute the work of a professional, and once again it is the fact that such 'work' is recorded in the files, never to be seen or challenged by the parents, that makes it so dangerous. And herein lies a power that professionals do not seem to realize they have got - to be the sole official judges of recent personal histories, to have their personal view of events elevated to the status of official records. The undesirable effects of this power can be seen in a number of ways. Firstly, the patronizing attitudes of some professionals are supported by the opportunities that professionals have to define parents who have been persuaded to change their minds as wayward sheep returning to the fold:

> "It was quite encouraging to see how aware they were of the need for X to have a somewhat wider range of demands placed upon her, by people who would not anticipate her every wish and over-interpret each gesture. They clearly feel (ESN(S) school) has now got something positive to offer X and were apologetic about not having got round to visiting it yet." - Files: Educational Psychologist.

Secondly, professionals may remind other professionals to persuade parents to make use of a service, and to make use of it in an appropriate way. This is particularly the case with the assessment hospital, where the availability, openness and flexibility of the service are all explained:

> "X's progress has been very good within the limits of her severe handicap and if a full review is required at any time this could be done at the (assessment unit). The upper age limit for the unit is eleven years, and the mother could visit the unit whenever she wishes." - Files: Assessment Unit.

The way the situation is set up stresses how natural and appropriate the service is, and given this pressure it is easy to see how parents who choose not to make use of the services come to be regarded as over-independent or even as troublemakers. This is because a third consequence of this power is to rule out the possibility of any alternative provision, and thus create a situation where parents looking for alternatives seem to be acting inappropriately.

> "Assessment so far indicates likely need for ESN(S) placement at ESN(S) school." - Files: Educational Psychologist.

> "The parents have promised to visit the hospital with Mr. A, Community Nurse, to see what can be arranged. I doubt if his care in a hostel would be feasible at present." - Files: Assessment Unit.

But perhaps the most dangerous consequence of this power to define how appropriate a service is, is to turn parental anxieties from reasonable reactions to situations into minor pathologies and create the possibility for such stereotyping as 'over-anxious mums' and 'handicapped families'.

The relationships between parents and professionals are therefore being managed with the aim of getting parents to accept the professionals' viewpoint. This will certainly cause problems for those parents whose strategy for coping with life is to treat their child as 'normally' as possible. But there does not appear to be much recognition of this in the attitude of some professionals to the services they administer, as the contradiction in this statement shows:

> "Her parents and brother show great affection for the child and are endeavouring to bring her up as normally as possible. They would welcome X's admission to (ESN(S) school)." - Files: source not clear.

Any attempts to bring up a child 'normally' are systematically undermined by segregated schooling, because what we mean by 'normal' schooling is itself dependent on the exclusion of certain categories of children ('slow-learners' as well as the mentally and physically-disabled). Similarly prolonged contact with hospital services, or the simple act of grouping handicapped people together are in themselves factors which work against what we would call 'normality'.

> "It is likely that he would benefit from being in a situation which can provide regular physiotherapy and be with children of a similar age and handicap." - Files: Paediatrician.

However, one danger is that by managing relationships in such ways, professionals will so begin to see special schools, for example, as logical places for certain children that such informal assumptions will pre-empt official and even statutory procedures:

> "She is due to start at (ESN(S) school) in May and we are going to arrange for an educational assessment to be performed in the near future." - Files: Doctor.

It seems to me that there is cause for genuine concern if the power of professionals becomes such that they cannot be bound by their own procedures.

If the professionals need to manage their relations with parents, then they do so in such a manner that the parents are far from sure how, why and when professionals are involved, or are supposed to be involved, with themselves and their child. Perhaps this has something to do with decreasing the ability of parents to judge situations for themselves, especially if the professionals fear their recommendations would not be taken up if parents knew too much and worried about decision-making (fieldwork diary). The lack of information that parents have sometimes emerges when paediatricians, uncertain what parents expect of them, are desperately searching for topics of conversation to fill up time in the clinic (Davis, A., 1982, p. 136):

> M   "Er .... he was under (medical officer) so I presume it's the same although I've not seen him for .../
> DR   Yes. What did he say? Did you have a discussion with him?
> M   I haven't seen him since X went to school .... Which is five years ago. Four years ago." - Paediatric clinic.

There seems to be something fundamentally anti-democratic in the apparent idea of some professionals that it is permissible to involve a service in decision-making about a child when firstly, that service has never seen the child, and secondly, when that service in being involved without the knowledge of the parents. I would like to suggest that it is keeping such involvement covert, rather than giving parents information, which is more likely to worry them. But it seems that once a child is in a special school, it becomes something of a clinical object, especially for the psychologists. But parents often do not know that their child is being seen by a psychologist at the school, or else do not know until after the meeting has taken place. Indeed, as a researcher I replicated this arrogance myself by using a meeting between a psychologist, a teacher and a child, as data without checking with the parents for permission. When I later told the parents of my involvement in such a meeting (of which they only knew afterwards) they were surprised and, very reasonably, not a little offended (fieldwork diary). The obvious danger is that one professional can involve another without the consent of the parents, and thereby impose a definition of the problem onto the parents, as with referring a case to Social Services without consulting the parents.

(e)   How Professionals Manage their Relationships with
      one another
One of the most important factors governing relationships between professionals is the idea that they represent a scarce resource and must be protected against any possible abuse and exploitation (Stimson and Webb, 1975, p. 59). We have already seen how, in the case of doctors particularly, this involves restricting the access that parents have to doctors, or 'gatekeeping'.

> "If it is felt in the future that the unit has a role to play in further assessments or treatments then application can be made through the usual channels." - Files: Medial officer.

This, of course, represents the formation of protective routines, and where, in given instances, doctors feel there is nothing else to be done, these routines become the focal points of their professional involvement:

> "I thought I would bring to your attention the fact that she has not had a regular paediatric review." - Files: Doctor.

The trouble is that whenever parents quite reasonably find such routines unhelpful or even troublesome and withdraw from them, this must then seem almost like an insult to the doctor concerned. But in recording the reaction of the parents to these routines it is the parents who are implicitly judged and insulted:

> "Mrs. X is extremely distraught because of X's behaviour and feels that nobody is interested in her problems or taking any notice of her. Nevertheless, she phoned to cancel her appointment today - this is the second cancelled appointment. When she is interested I will arrange to see her myself next time." - Files: Paediatrician.

One might have more respect for the doctors' position here were they somewhat less cynical about the value of such routines, as we shall see in chapter 5 (p. 166). On the other hand some doctors are well aware that the routine paediatric review can be troublesome, unhelpful and a constant reminder of the stigma that parents and child have to bear.

> "I assume that the parents quite reasonably feel that paediatric outpatient appointments are superfluous." - Files: Doctor.

> "I will cancel this (i.e. a clinic with one particular child) as I think it damaging often for parents of these badly handicapped children to see too many doctors." - Files: Paediatrician.

But it is only when a more senior consultant (from a regional hospital, for example) is involved, and the position of protecting themselves from potential exploitation is removed, that these more considerate sentiments can emerge. However, where the priority is felt to be the need to protect oneself and other doctors from accusations and so on, then doctors will not be prepared to criticize other doctors. This detracts from the best interests of parents and child in several ways. Firstly, types of treatment which may well have their limitations may be defended for the sake of professional relationships:

> DR "They're not only ineffective but, you know, you can get symptoms and side effects from the antibiotics themselves.
> F That's right, yes. He lives quite a lot on antibiotics.

M   Oh, yes. Well, he's never off them.
DR   So the family doctor prescribes them frequently does he?
F   Yes.
DR   Yes .... well I mean sometimes ..... that's er .. indicated and necessary." - Paediatric clinic.

Secondly, this defence may well be taking up a doctor's time and energy, which as scarce resources, could be better spent in addressing the problems the parents and child have got. And thirdly, this represents yet another front on which the energies of the parents are to be sapped in struggling to see to their child's interests. Similarly, a doctor may seek to defend a related profession that is coming in for a certain amount of criticism by suggesting that the child be referred to that service:

DR   "Does X ever have any physiotherapy?
M   No he doesn't have anything. Just whatever they do at school with him.
DR   What we could do would be to get him assessed by our occupational therapist here.
M   Mmn.
DR   There's a/I think that things will start to improve, um, before very long. Because the occupational therapy department has got er a new boss really and she's very keen to sort of/services for children.
M   Oh, I see.
DR   Well, we could contact her." - Paediatric clinic.

But when the mother has heard nothing four months later (fieldwork diary), one possibility is that the most important consideration in the suggestion was the management of professional relationships, rather than any real determination to get therapy for the child.

Another influence on the way in which doctors relate to one another is that each is a representative of a specialist knowledge and must be free to make decisions independently without interference. This influence is no doubt strengthened by the need to be deferential to those

higher up the medical hierarchy, however incompetent
they might be. It appears that the interests of protecting
relationships between medical professionals come before
the interests of the parent or the mentally-handicapped
child which might logically require interference or
criticism of a doctor:

> DR "So (local specialist) is going to look at
> him to/
> M He's seeing him Thursday afternoon, yes.
> So um ..... I don't know whether you can
> make/recommend anything as well or
> whether it's just him.
> DR Once (local specialist) is involved I think
> perhaps no. Because he doesn't like, er,
> some people telling him what to do and
> (other things. He says, I'm expected to do
> (my job, so let me do my job.
> (M No, I think this is ....
> (......... Yes, yes.
> DR I've been in trouble sometimes in the
> past.
> M Oh, I see. (laughs)
> DR So now I will not enter in that field."
> - Paediatric clinic.

And whilst one professional is not prepared to criticize
another the problems of parents and child remain undealt
with. If the parents seek to make the criticisms
themselves, then professionals may try to protect those
professionals who they fear may become scapegoats.

> "(Parents') current dissatisfaction with services
> has perhaps for them been focussed on this
> particular nurse. Occasionally individuals in the
> helping professions bear the brunt of criticisms
> from parents which are really criticisms of the
> services." - Files: Psychologist.

At the same time that professionals may want (or expect
the parents to want) to leave the responsibility for
decision-making to themselves, they are keen to avoid
taking responsibility for their own actions. For example,
many parents consider physiotherapy help appropriate and
even vital for their child. However, provision is very much

lacking, and this fact is sadly and repeatedly discussed in the various meetings between professionals and parents. The appropriateness of the missing service can be judged by the way that physiotherapy help in the past is wistfully remembered:

> M   "(Physiotherapist) came and she sort of made lots of quite simple suggestions, which, when you're in the know, um/just with little things like getting X down steps." - Paediatric clinic.

The importance of this service may also be inferred by the way that what little help is still available highlights the tragic consequences of the continuing lack of physiotherapy support.

> T   "And the objective, they want to help him to get extension of his arms. Um (physiotherapist) said it _is_ possible. It's got to be done very, very slowly. But she said, it's bad because they've always been in this position and haven't been moved that they're not straight. They should be." - Educational case-conference.

Now doctors obviously cannot be held responsible for the overall level of finance that health services receive. But the medical profession as a whole does have some responsibility in the allocation of priorities, and in influencing paramedical professions. The high status enjoyed within the profession by technological, acute, hospital-centred concerns not only denies funds to areas such as mental handicap and therapy, but also encourages therapy professionals to lead their discipline to look to similar concerns as they themselves struggle for higher status. And even doctors involved with handicap are responsible to the extent that they see what is actually an important resource for disabled children as trivial or inappropriate. One doctor wondered out loud to me what was the point of physiotherapy for children who were never going to walk anyway (fieldwork diary), ignoring entirely its uses in enabling children to lie or sit comfortably, to preventing increasing deformities, or to achieve partial control of limbs in order to be able to communicate through signs. Another doctor had an incredibly patronizing view of the expertise that therapists possess:

> DR   "Don't think that the occupational therapist or physiotherapist or somebody, they are expert (...) There is no difference. And they learned it from somebody. So you are to learn from them and start doing it. Best thing to do." - Paediatric clinic.

The danger, of course, is that in managing relations between themselves and other professionals, doctors will fail to recognize the value of such services as therapy, and the access that children will have to such services will be incidental, even accidental, when they should be as rights.

CONCLUSION

The argument of this chapter has been that services to parents and handicapped children can themselves be the cause of many problems for these parents and children.

The technical and acute emphasis of medical knowledge may mean parents and child continuing to attend paediatric clinics which can offer little, whilst not having access to therapy which can offer much. Developmental testing and assessments in hospital are not experiences so-called 'normal' children have to endure, yet the reasonable reactions of parents and children to these special experiences are recorded as the 'facts' of professional knowledge. Eventually the mere fact of being in contact with certain services becomes seen as a confirmation that the child is handicapped.

Even though they may be aware of the stress it causes, doctors who are anxious about their lack of knowledge may see routine clinics and assessments as the only thing they can offer. Parents then feel frustrated in their attempts to be critical because something has apparently been done, even though nothing substantive may have been achieved. If the parents then feel unable to criticize the professionals, it may be that bureaucratic requirements and fear of complaint will provide a continued impetus for the existence of such routines. But such routines can also prove a block to other sources of help such as therapy. The inability to see problems in terms other than the limits to their own knowledge means that professionals will have fixed assumptions about the way parents should respond to their circumstances. And since a further way of doing what little they can is to record problems in their files, the result is that popular and stigmatizing stereotypes of the parents and child will be recorded as 'facts'. Not only this, but the issue for the professionals actually becomes how 'appropriately' parents respond to services. But in fact it is most likely that parents will <u>not</u> react as professionals hope precisely because of the limits to what professionals know and can do, and because of the relative expertise of the mother with regard to her own child. This in turn encourages the dangerous precedent of professionals not realizing their own power and not consulting with parents about decisions.

In fact there are differences between parents about how much responsibility they want in making decisions. But professionals assume <u>all</u> parents want to give up this responsibility and therefore presume to dictate to organized groups of parents how they should behave, thus denying possibly the greatest potential source of knowledge. Professionals therefore expect parents to follow their instructions, and recording instances where parents decline to do so means that the files read as criticisms of the parents which the parents cannot challenge. To simply ask the parents when they wanted contact from services would seem to go against the notion that being a professional means being in control. This makes dealing with services a very fraught experience for parents if decisions are handed down to them from 'on high' which frustrate their attempts to bring their child up 'normally'.

Managing their relationships with parents to prevent being exploited as a scarce resource will mean firstly that the real problem of parents and child will be lost amidst the routine questioning, and secondly, that services will be arranged in ways which help professionals' management, and not necessarily in the best interests of parents and child. Professionals worry about parents having access to alternative resources which could provide them with information to challenge the decisions of professionals. If professionals, in anticipating a challenge to decisions, use files as an aggressive form of protection, then these may appear as character attacks on the parents. Putting the assumption that parents have not told them everything to the centre of their strategy for managing relations becomes another way in which professional stereotypes can be inadvertently imposed on families. And with the files comes the power to put one's own personal gloss on the recording of events - the assumption that the professional view is correct, that services should be used in certain ways they deem 'appropriate', that 'there is no alternative' to these services and that parents' reactions can be labelled reasonable or pathological. But the most dangerous power is that when professionals cannot even be bound by their own procedures, and when services are involved without parents' permission, or even knowledge.

In managing relations between one another, professionals seem to establish routines, with parents judged depending on their reaction to these routines. More humane attitudes prevail only in the absence of such routines. And whilst professionals are prepared to put their 'good relations' above the possible need to criticize other professionals, then the best interests of parents and child may suffer. Similarly, doctors can be held responsible if they misuse the power they have relative to a less powerful profession in such a way as to deny a much-needed therapy service for disabled children.

It appears that some services provided for parents of mentally-handicapped children are not necessarily to their advantage. In engaging with the services, the parents lose the possibility of becoming aware of, and using, a whole set of resources. These include self-confidence and a sense of control over one's own life; time to address problems on one's own terms; money which is used up in professionally-centred services; strength which is reduced in the struggle against inappropriate services; and information which is hidden from parents. It could be that by withdrawing from inappropriate or irrelevant contact with the services (routine paediatric recalls, assessments that achieve nothing, testing that is not linked to a practical solution, encounters that offer no more than a friendly chat), this would give the parents more control, time, money and energy to deal with issues as they see them. It would also remove some of the burden of work from the professionals, give them more time so that they could become more client-centred and impart accurate information at the crucial stages.

Chapter Five

OBTAINING INFORMATION

PROBLEMS OF INFORMATION: PARENTAL INTERVIEWS

Two issues in particular are considered in relation to the parental interviews. When are parents kept informed and when are they not? And how is information withheld from parents both intentionally and unintentionally?

(a) When information is, or is not, given to parents
The first point to note is simply that parents appreciate being given information about their child. It seems that openness on the part of a professional increases the respect that a parent holds for that professional:

> M   "We went back to (paediatrician). He had a copy of the report and our doctor did. In fact our doctor told us more .... than (paediatrician) did at the time. Our doctor's very good actually. He doesn't hide things from you. He'll tell you."

Information can also emerge from a situation where parents of disabled children can use one another's experience as a resource. Three parents said that they appreciated the meetings recently initiated by social workers in the area, which aimed to give them information about the services and benefits available to the children. But such meetings also open up the opportunity for parents to inform one another:

    M   "It's awful when you've first got a child like this because you don't know anybody and this is why (social worker) is starting these meetings as well. Just to introduce you to other parents (....) We didn't know anybody with a young child that you could discuss your problems with. 'Cause we think that's more important than anything, with a handicapped child, to be able to talk to somebody else who's got the same problem."

Parents who have not experienced these meetings may also stress the importance of other parents as the most reliable source of information.

    F   "The only information you get is from parents (...) And our phone bill is pretty high because we ring parents with handicapped children. 'Have you heard about this? Have you been there? Have you done this?' You're not told by the government or anything else. You just hear it through other parents."

Indeed, only three parents in all felt that they had received good information from the services. And useful information emerges for very specific reasons, perhaps, for example, because a doctor has been prompt in referring parents on to relevant services. More typical are the parents who say that they received no information from the professionals on how they might best manage their child. However, it is not just the lack of information which may concern the parents. Their anxiety may be increased by not knowing why they are denied access to certain information, such as the files kept by the professionals on the children.

    M   "There was quite a lengthy report. But the thing was we were never allowed to see the report (...) We never had/I don't know is it medical/because of medical practice that parents don't read these things?"

Or when they are denied information through being excluded from case-conferences they may not be satisfied or convinced by the explanation they are given:

M   "They do have a case-conference after they've been in. Which I think parents should be allowed in on, but they're not allowed in on it (....) They think that the parents wouldn't understand the medical terms and that, but I still think that you should be allowed in <u>anyway</u>, whether you understand it or not, you know, as a parent anyway."

Moreover, there is some suggestion that lack of information does not only make parents anxious, but it also leads them to be distrusting of information they do receive, even to the extent of undermining the very possibility of maintaining a relationship with the professionals:

F   "I think a lot of them are two-faced to be quite honest. They say one thing to you and then say other things behind your back.
(...)
I don't think they're very, you know, frank enough with you."

But even when parents <u>do</u> have access to information this does not in itself tell us anything about the struggle involved in obtaining such information. Several of the parents interviewed felt that they had had to push and fight to gain what little information they now had:

M   "Everything that you had to do for that child, <u>you</u> had to do. The facilities were there, and once we found the facilities they were marvellous. <u>But</u> if you weren't the pushy type/sometimes I think that I turned into a shrew (laughs) But if you weren't the pushy type, there was so much you never found out and never learned."

Other parents felt that they only knew the information

they did because they had been fortunate in some way.

> M   "We were quite lucky in that I was a nurse before I had the children so I tended to know, even if I didn't know the details of who to get in touch with, I'd got an idea of what services there were about."

A few parents even thought that they lacked certain information even though they were in contact with the relevant services.

> M   "I mean at the hospital when you go to see the paediatrician. If there is something wrong with your child and they know, they should tell you, or there should be leaflets there at the clinics to pick up which is easier (...) I mean there's offices up there, social workers. You should be directed straight up there without coming home. I mean there are facilities, but you never know of them, do you?"

It is the ways in which information does not smoothly follow from contact with the services that is dealt with below.

(b)   How information is (unintentionally) not given
There seem to be many ways in which parents may feel themselves to be obstructed by a lack of information at times when professionals may feel they are informing the parents. Sometimes the information is inaccurate in such a way that it hinders the emergence of relevant information. Some parents said that they had been given information about their child's disability which was subsequently shown to be incorrect:

> M   "We took X for hearing tests and the staff weren't very nice at all. Because X, as a child, he screamed a lot. I mean we know now that this was part of his handicap, you know, his screaming and that. But they sort of dismissed him as a

> thoroughly disruptive, spoilt, only child, you know. Take him away, sort of thing, we can't do anything with him. So we never got any hearing tests done properly. And the doctor said, well we <u>think</u> he's deaf. How they came to that conclusion I do not know but 'we think he's deaf.'"

Other parents had been wrongly denied access to benefits through poor or inaccurate information:

> M "I did go to the Welfare Rights (...) She said you could apply to the Family Fund, you know, the Rowntree. But usually, she said, there's only you two and X and your husband's got a job - whether you'd get it or not I don't know (...) I did think of putting in for the night allowance (...) but they put me off there. The Welfare Rights people, I did ask them about that and she said, 'I very much doubt you'll get that,' she said, 'it's very hard to get'."

Even in cases where parents may have information on which to act, this may be undermined by contradictory information from the professionals, which, as in this example, later proved to be incorrect:

> M "We had this sort of thing that perhaps physiotherapy would help her (...) 'cause at the time it was sort of her limbs, she just wasn't't/They <u>looked</u> perfectly normal but they just didn't go where they were supposed to. And, um, the doctors kept saying, 'everything you're doing is right, that's all you can do'."

Another way in which information may unintentionally not be communicated concerns the amount of time that is spent giving parents that information. Parents felt that an insufficient amount of time had been spent in explaining the nature of the child's disability to them. A further complication to the process of giving parents information is that professionals may not distinguish (perhaps because they themselves do not realize) between opinion and fact:

> M   "We put no limitations on him and we
> won't allow anybody else to do it either.
> I was accused by a doctor once of having
> my head in the sand like an ostrich,
> refusing to see certain things. Now I
> know as of today, he might be restricted
> in lots of ways. But that is today. That is
> not to say that he'll be that way in six
> months' time or twelve months' time or
> in two years' time. Because six months
> ago we brought a child here who was
> lying on the floor and could do nothing.
> Now we've got a child who is almost
> fully mobile. So I won't allow anyone to
> put him in a little box and label him."

When professionals try to give parents information there is
sometimes the danger that parents may not hear the
advice, and that more than one meeting may be needed to
explain the situation to them. Thus information may
inadvertently not be communicated if it is only given by
word of mouth and not written down, or if it is only
repeated once. Several parents said that they had
forgotten or not taken in information properly at the first
attempt:

> M   "Yes, you do get a shock but you don't
> get it all at once. Because I don't really
> believe your brain takes it in anyway.
> Because afterwards the paediatrician said
> well I explained this and that and the
> other to you when I first told you about
> the fact he'd got to have a heart repair.
> And I said to him, you didn't. And he
> said, but I did. And he probably did. But
> you see your brain only takes in what it
> can. And you cope as it comes."

However, even when the parents have received and
understood the information this does not represent the end
to their troubles. It may be that much of the information
that they receive particular parents may find unhelpful, or
at least extremely limited. Three parents mentioned that

they had received a vague 'carry on as usual' line as advice on child management. A number of parents had been given information which they felt to be unhelpful, and certainly to an outside observer such comments appear unconstructive:

> M   "I think (paediatrician)'s one thing was that they can save these children at birth which they did X (....) And I don't think he thought .... some of them should have been saved. Because it was up to him to deal with them afterwards. And I think that was ... his sort of view (...) He knew, I think, what sort of life we were going to have with him. And in his way he felt it kinder to let X go."

Closely related to these instances is the fact that information will often be seen as unhelpful when it is presented as the only alternative, or else when no alternative is suggested:

> F   "See now, we didn't listen to all these experienced doctors: you know, he's dead, that's it, finished. Before that they said he was dying, they said take him home to die."

Similarly, one set of parents had successfully weaned their child off anti-convulsant drugs which had been prescribed for a child who had never had a fit, to the obvious dismay of professionals for whom drugs seem to be an essential part of child management (Schrag and Divoky, 1981).

> F   "Every time you take her anywhere they say 'what drugs is she on?' She's not on drugs. 'She's not on drugs?!' Doesn't make sense. It's the answer in this country - it's pills, drugs."

Such are the ways in which information is not given for reasons that seem to be relatively unintentional. But there also appear to be certain times when information is intentionally not communicated, for a number of reasons.

(c) When information is (intentionally) not given
One of the ways in which to withhold information is to only give the parents a partial or insufficient explanation of the circumstances. After all, a doctor may very well be anxious about being blamed for being the messenger of bad news:

> M   "It wasn't until I had him, until he was born. And they came up and they said he had a lump on the back of the neck, well, or on the head. Well I didn't know anything about that then. I mean, I didn't know that spina bifida was even thought of."

Likewise, even when told specifically about certain government allowances, parents encountered problems because of the detailed aspects of the allowances about which they had not been told (especially at times of cut-backs professionals may assume that they have the right to be the guardian of the state's purse). This means that parents may only be told about an allowance years after they become entitled to it. Also, they may not be told how to cope with the interview which precedes any recognition of a right to the attendance allowance, nor how to challenge or appeal against a decision which goes against them. Finally, pride in self-sufficiency or independence may mean that a number of claimants are put off pursuing their rights to benefits unless they realize that many parents in similar situations are claiming:

> M   "We had to fight to get the full allowance for him. They say it's not a means test and we know for a fact that one of them was a means test when they came. Because they actually admitted when they came back. We fought for two years to get full allowance. And he must have been seven before I got it. And we hadn't had a night's sleep since we had him. But how can you prove it to them? (...) They put you in such a position you feel as if you're, you know, asking for charity. And I didn't want it. But it's not until you're with other people, and you

> realize, well you're entitled to it. You know, it's not just something they're giving you, you know it's an entitlement."

Furthermore, it seems strange that GPs, who know little about handicap, help judge the entitlement of parents of handicapped children to the attendance allowance. The effect of withholding information by giving only partial explanations is compounded if the explanation is made in an insensitive manner. Parents continue to report that the way they had been told about the child's handicap had been insensitive:

> M   "Well (doctor) hadn't said anything to me and then he just said um words to the effect don't go congratulating yourself there's something the matter."

Information is also effectively being withheld when restricted expressions or professional jargon are used. In fact three parents felt that they had not understood the information they had been given for one of these two reasons:

> F   "He sat X on the table and he held her and he picked up a book. And he started turning the pages over. That's it, he said. (Name of syndrome). So we said, what's that? He said, oh it's er it's .... something wrong with X. We said, well what is it? You wouldn't understand if I told you, he said."

Doctors may decide to hold information back in the sense that they do not tell the parents about the diagnosis together. This appears to be a deliberate strategy to avoid giving information, perhaps to reduce the doctor's anxiety in imparting bad news, as this sometimes involves directing the mother that she should tell the father about the diagnosis. Parents complained when they were not given information together.

It is perhaps for similar reasons that doctors in particular adopt what has been called a 'wait and see' policy with regard to certain information-giving (see Stacey, 1980, pp. 82 and 87). This applies in particular to the suspicions a doctor may have about the possibility of a child's disability. By not informing the parents of any suspicions a doctor may mislead a parent anxious to know whether or not her child is all right. Parents felt that they had not been kept informed such that they did not understand the reason behind the procedures involved:

> M   "It's funny because we've just started a group up - parents of handicapped children. And none of the parents can actually put down and say what did the doctor say before you found out the child was handicapped. None of us can remember them ever saying anything. I mean I used to go up (to the hospital) I think it was every six months with X. But I thought that was because he was premature, being so small just/for his development of his body. And put it down to that."

The vast majority of parents felt that they had not been informed as soon as possible about the suspected diagnosis of their child's condition:

> M   "I should think it was when she was coming up for eight or nine months that we decided that something was wrong. But she was a little older when the doctors acknowledged that although the ..... variations in normal were great, she was sort of gradually slipping behind.
>
> F   She was over a year before they actually said anything was really wrong, didn't they?"

It is clear that parents have anxieties and suspicions of their own which they sometimes feel are not listened to by the doctors. Nearly half the parents had had their anxieties aroused by the procedures of the professionals before the diagnosis is given. In such circumstances a 'wait and see' approach will only increase the parents' anxiety and stress, even if this means the parents can be told less bluntly:

M "The family doctor ..... picked her up and looked at her and her tongue was big, was very big. For the size that she was (...) He kept looking at her and moving her tongue and moving her fingers. And he said: 'oh, she's got joints missing off her little fingers.' Well we didn't take any particular notice and he never said anything. And then when the time came for my post-natal in six weeks, he said bring the baby down. So I went down and I took X. Any by this time I really, really thought that there was something wrong."

But the unfortunate consequences of this conscious strategy of withholding information do not end with parental stress and anxiety. Whilst doctors 'wait and see', entitlement to government benefits slips by. Several of the parents complained that they were only told about government benefits at a late stage.

GM "I mean if we'd known about that (attendance allowance) right from the start we could have had it two years earlier. But they don't tell you nothing about that do they? It's amazing what you find out, you know, when you've been through it."

Similarly, of the three couples in the study who had received genetic counselling, two had other children before the information was given, partly as a consequence of a 'wait and see' strategy.

F "(Paediatrician) got in the specialist, I can't remember his name now, um .... genetic specialist, and he gave us the chances of having another handicapped child which was too late by the time they did it because we'd already got (X's sister).

M (laughs) Who was all right.

F It was one of those slow/you know, took the National Health so long to do it we'd got another one anyhow.

137

> M   No, in fairness to them they/<u>it was only</u>
> <u>after</u> (paediatrician) said, yes he thought
> <u>X would be slow that he then made us an</u>
> <u>appointment</u>." (My emphasis)

It is clear that information, which could and should be a major resource for parents of handicapped children, is denied in a variety of intentional and unintentional ways. The information is often not given at all. In other cases it is inaccurate; partial; insensitively phrased; late; given to parents separately; only given after suspicions and anxieties have been aroused; given once only; only given verbally; given in terms that are confusing or jargon that is not understood. Furthermore, sometimes the information that is given is in itself unhelpful; no alternative is presented; opinion and fact are not distinguished, and important additional details are missed out when the information is about government benefits.

FILES AND MEETINGS

This section deals with the way in which issues of information are dealt with by professionals in files and meetings.

(a)   Professional Knowledge

There have been some arguments presented in favour of requiring professionals to be open and frank in giving parents information. However, because of the many moral, social and political aspects of professional knowledge that are obscured by techniques and routines, to inform parents adequately (so that they could base their decisions on the widest possible knowledge) would involve opening up a whole range of issues, about which the professionals themselves are probably not aware. In the following extract a senior clinical medical officer explains the use of the Griffiths Developmental Test to a mother. But the explanation fails to consider what the political consequences are of focussing on certain children by such testing (see Chapter 3, pp. 36-40 and Chapter 4, pp. 91-4); what social factors are presupposed by any of the individual test items; what is socially specific about our ideas of 'normality'; what the social implications are of <u>any</u>

concept of normality, and whether any of these social factors are politically tolerable. In addition, from the point of view of the mother, to be told that her five-year-old son has a mental age of 21 months is an indication firstly that the doctors were wrong to 'write off' her child and that her belief that he could be more intelligent than he was is justified, and secondly that her belief was more than borne out since he had improved despite a multiplicity of physical disabilities, operations and periods in hospital. In view of this one must question how far this admittedly frank, detailed and well-meaning account is contributing to a genuine informing of the mother. It is the beginning to a series of more complex problems, not an end in itself:

M	"I'm intrigued by your test .... I'm intrigued by what ..... putting shapes together and different patterns in their correct holes. What exactly does it tell you?
DR	What does it tell me? Well, one knows that .... you know these things have been worked out on lots of children. And we know that children of certain ages should be able to do certain things. And what one is trying to work out is what is X's/
M	Mental age.
DR	Mental age.
M	Right.
DR	What level he is working at in different things.
M	And what would you say his mental age was?
DR	Well the overall one that comes out is about 21 months .... I think he/ Well, he's undoubtedly higher 24, 25 months on the personal-social (scale). That's/you know, that's the way he can start to feed himself in certain things.
M	Yes.
DR	Um .... knowing parts of the body, opening the door. He's coming out at about/just about 24 months there. Building the tower, when he got up to the eight bricks, um .... those kind of

things and what/and where he's doing
with his scribbles; throwing a ball, again
about 24 months. Putting the ... six
shapes back in the board with/just in the
minute, is taking him to 25, 26 months.
Now if he was rather more co-operative
today we may have got him another
month or two on.

M Yes.

DR But/and then/overall .... he's 21.5
months I'd say and his age is 65 months,
so we give you a/his mental age as a
percentage of his actual age and it's 33
per cent.

M Right.

DR And when I saw him last time it was 33
per cent.

M So up.

DR So that means/

M He's keeping up.

DR He's going along at the steady rate ....
The first time I saw him he was 28 per
cent and that was before he went to
school.

M Yes.

DR So going to school has .... helped him
along, and he's progressing steadily." -
Visit by medical officer.

In fact it appears that the doctor himself is unaware of
the social and logical controversies in what he is saying.
Indeed, this may partly explain why, when trying to inform
the mother about the nature of the child's disability, his
explanations slide over into labelling or unnecessarily
limiting (not to mention insulting) the child.

M "My mother saw him 14 months ago, so I
don't have to tell you what (improvement)
she sees in him.

DR She saw him ..... well, not quite a
cabbage. (half laughs)" - Visit by medical
officer.

The emphasis of medical knowledge on causes will
mean that information on a child's diagnosis may mean

different things to the parents than to the doctors, when parents see retardation as an outcome of disabilities and doctors see disabilities as evidence or confirmation of a generalized retardation: "Retarded development as part of the syndrome." - Files: Medical officer.

Doctors appear to see the aetiology of a disability as crucial to, or even as constituting their knowledge. They seem to implicitly communicate to some parents the view that the social dimension of the problem consists in filling in the gaps in medical knowledge by increased emphasis on medical research, though not all parents are willing to accept this rather narrow view unquestioningly:

>F "And of course no-one has been able to tell us why, why it happened, why he was born like that. Well, you know, that's something we don't know yet.
>
>M I haven't met a mother who knows (...) Nobody I've ever met has known why it happened.
>
>SMD Is that the most important question? (...)
>
>M Oh, I couldn't care less! (...) That's almost the first question that doctors ask you (...) They always want to know why. They say, did you have a temperature? (...) Because, you see it's part of their research, I guess. (...) You've got to get on with it. You've got to get on with living, not what might have been." - Interview.

And so, beyond identifying the supposed cause of a disability and giving the parents this diagnosis, there is a gap where the doctors may be uncertain what else is expected of them. Information about child management seems to be secondary to this concern about diagnosis in a number of ways. Without a known diagnosis doctors may lose their whole orientation to the case, with issues of management restricted to private exchanges between professionals:

>"I have had a number of investigations done and none of them have shown any abnormality. I would be grateful for your help with the

> management of his handicap." - Files: Doctor.

At best this may mean that information may be little more than kindly encouragement. Indeed, this may be enough if child management is going relatively well for the parents. However, a more disquieting side to this orientation on the part of the doctor is that the vacuum is filled by information and advice which the parents find unhelpful:

> "I tried to reinforce your feeling that active steps should he deteriorate would not be justifiable." - Files: Doctor.

Indeed drug therapies may be used which prove to be unhelpful, whilst at the same time the parents do not know the uncertainties and suspicions which surround such therapies which are offered because the doctor may not want to increase the parents' anxiety and/or considers control of such information to be a matter of professional discretion (see Stimson and Webb, 1975, p. 128):

> "It seems he was quite aggressive at school which was probably the effect of Ritalen." Files: Doctor.

What the various doctors write in the files about diagnosing disabilities also gives an indication of why the parents experience difficulties with information given at the time of diagnosis. For example, there are four cases in the group of twenty where the medical diagnosis is Down's Syndrome. With such a well-known and well-documented condition there is a danger that the outcome of the disability is mechanically deduced from the syndrome. Thus severe subnormality is still seen as a necessary consequence of Down's Syndrome despite the fact that in terms of tests which claim to measure intelligence, many would only be labelled moderately retarded. More important than this, however, is the unnecessary social handicapping that may be associated with the diagnosis. Firstly, in that implicitly making a link between ranked intelligence and social possibilities, the social world of a Down's child is artificially limited. And secondly, the issue of medical scrutiny must be set in a context where there is a general under-estimation of the relative stupidity of the rest of the population who are not subject to such close investigation (see Chapter 4, pp. 91-4). When the diagnosis of a syndrome or condition is relatively straightforward the problem of information associated with diagnosis will be in distinguishing necessary as opposed to socially-determined outcomes of a disability. The danger is that the doctor, and other professionals, may confuse the two, as in this example where both the parents and the teachers are convinced that the child is in fact severely physically disabled and intelligent:

> "Diagnosis: Myoclonic epilepsy, severe subnormality."
> - Files: Paediatrician.

(b) Limits to Professional Knowledge

In a certain sense, the problem of parents receiving adequate information is a problem misconceived since the parents are the real experts on their own child. Here a mother has to remind a senior clinical medical officer who is trying to test the child, that the child is severely hearing-impaired. From the context of the rest of the encounter it seems more likely the doctor does not know/has forgotten the child is hearing-impaired rather than has assumed the hearing aid to be in.

> DR   "X! ....X! Where is your nose? Will he/does he know parts of the body?
> M   He does, he does. According to the report I got from school. But I'm just sitting here wondering how much of it he's been/he hasn't got his hearing aid on." - Visit by medical officer.

The way in which parents actually provide the professionals with their information is then extended when the mother gives the senior clinical medical officer the information estimating the child's level of ability so that the doctor can complete his tests. But the 'information' he then gives the mother sounds somewhat absurd. He has to be reminded the child is deaf, he has to rely largely on the mother's information about what the child can do only to come up with the world-shattering conclusion that the tests show that the child is handicapped with regard to hearing and speech:

DR   "If one set a few things in front of him .... a doll, a ball, a spoon, and things and said: 'give me the ball', would he do it?

M   Errr ..... now. They've been doing this (at school). It's all connected with his hearing.

DR   Yes.

M   They were working on this for a couple of years with his hearing. And if he sort of/oh, again, in the mood, yes he can do it. Provided there aren't too many things in front of him.

DR   Yes. That's right.

M   If I have about three things.

DR   Mmn.

M   But I couldn't say a hundred out of a hundred, no.

DR   No .... OK. So what is really coming through from this testing and what you've shown me and told me is how handicapped he is on the hearing and speech side." - Visit by medical officer.

However, the information the mother continues to provide reaches the point where the role of the senior clinical medical officer is becoming entirely upstaged and he is reduced to the defeated exclamation 'Oh!' This, coupled with the fact that hearing-impairment, which was not an issue until the mother pointed it out, has now become an all-embracing explanation, suggests that this very explanation represents a somewhat desperate attempt to regain some credibility:

M   "Um, are you aware that he had a paralysed right vocal chord? None of us were until (date) when they operated on his heart. (laughs)

DR   Oh.

M   And they said/the ENT people said that that would have a lot to do with the fact he's not talking yet.

DR   I would have thought that the hearing is more .....

M   Yes.

DR   Personally.

M   Yes.

DR   I think if you are deaf. You can't hear and therefore you can't respond." - Visit by medical officer.

Furthermore, parents who join together in groups and associations may well develop a more appropriate stock of information than the doctors, leading to the type of situation where a mother approaches a doctor for advice when that doctor knows only as much or even less than the mother herself:

DR   "Are you a member of the Down's Association?

M   Yes, yes.

DR   Have .... is there any sort of um .... knowledge within that group about this?" - Paediatric clinic.

Paediatricians seem in some instances to be very aware of the limits to medical knowledge in dealing with disability. Often they may wonder precisely what they can tell parents, and so they make the most of the opportunities they do have to give the parents the type of information which the parents find appropriate, and to give it in a manner which the parents find useful:

DR   "Yes, I thought/As I say, I thought it was what's called an innocent murmur.

M   Ah!

DR   And that is that it/it's just/You can hear blood being squeezed through the heart and out of the heart. And that means the heart's normal." - Paediatric clinic.

The usefulness of such information is based on the following assumption, namely that the doctor feels he has to offer the parents some kind of information, even if it seems boring or routine, in order to reassure them. One paediatrician addressed the following remark to me at the very beginning of a clinic that I was taping:

DR   "You don't mind how frivolous it may be? Because that's part of the business of

> making certain people aren't worrying." -
> Paediatric clinic.

However, the degree of usefulness of the information to
the parents will vary according to the context in which
the information emerges, and so too will the extent to
which information is a reassurance or irritation to the
parents. From the parental interviews it is clear that
there is a varying degree of reassurance which parents
derive from the doctor keeping the parent informed about
the routine checks and procedures he has made with
regard to the child.

> DR   "Yes, now, er, what about his haemoglobin?
> We've done that at some stage. Yes, here
> we are. That's a little bit down. 12.8
> grams. Little bit of anaemia there. Er ....
> but his iron level isn't too bad. It's 16." -
> Paediatric clinic.

Factors which will tend to decrease the value of such
information from the parents' point of view include the
continued repetition of such checks over a number of
years; where the diagnosis is known, or not known but not
considered important; where the parents are using a
strategy based on bringing up their child as normally as
possible, or where the child does not suffer regular
illnesses associated with the disability.

Meanwhile, the doctors may feel uneasy at the
prospect of admitting the limits to their knowledge
directly because they quite correctly estimate that
parents expect medical knowledge to be complete and a
hundred per cent effective. Probably neither the doctors
nor the parents are aware of the extent to which control
of a problem may precede the knowledge and that
knowledge of a problem does not mean it can be
controlled. But to the extent that doctors use this
impression of complete knowledge as a rhetorical
justification for clinical control and social privilege, one
cannot really symphathize with the problems they then
face. Such a problem arises in the following example from
a paediatric clinic. The mother's account has involved
detailed examples of how in certain instances her child
demonstrates intelligent behaviour, and the reply comes:

> DR "No, I can't explain that." - Paediatric clinic.

I feel that this is intended not so much as an admission of a lack of knowledge, so much as a strategy based on the perception (expressed explicitly in the corresponding file) that the parents have not 'accepted' the child's disability. The doctor 'cannot explain' the child's intelligent behaviour because it is an anomaly with his ESN(S) status. This seems to point to reasons why doctors may prefer deception to an admission that they do not know what is wrong with the child. Firstly, the doctors will have difficulty in reconciling the logically, if not empirically, contradictory themes that they do not know the diagnosis and that the parents have not accepted the nature of the child's disability. As one mother put it:

> M "They didn't know what was wrong with him, but he would always be like it. Now our argument was, if you don't know what's wrong with him, how do you know he's always going to be like it?" - Interview.

From the doctor's point of view a clear, informative statement of their lack of knowledge leaves them very open to the mother's argument above. Secondly, by leaving the statement about their lack of knowledge until the child is much older, the doctors can implicitly point to the child's lack of progress, thus overcoming the apparent contradiction between having no diagnosis to offer and wanting the parents to accept a professional viewpoint on the nature of their child's disability. When doctors do give some indication to parents about how their knowledge is limited, it is clear that the limitation comes from the very orientation of medical knowledge. In this case it was only useful when the child was very young and then only when the child had a specific physical medical problem that could be dealt with.

> DR "It's strange the memories you have of people. And I/I just remember X (aged 10) as being a baby. I mean not because she hasn't grown up or developed or anything but because that's just/You

147

> know, that's/I suppose that's my (inaudible)
> medical ethic." - Paediatric clinic.

One of the apparent consequences of such limits to medical knowledge is that having little to offer, the thoughts of doctors turn to concern over their relationship with parents. Now if it is true that "doctors' own 'devious' control strategies with regard to the imparting of information are seen by them to be a matter for the discretion of the individual doctor, and are a legitimate means of managing the patient and building up a 'proper' or 'good' relationship with him" (Stimson and Webb, 1975, p. 128), then doctors may consider that part of their 'discretion' is to look at the reaction of parents to information they may have been given. Sometimes the reaction of parents may meet with professional approval, particularly if it is deferential to the power of professional medical knowledge.

> "I was very impressed by the attitude and skill of
> the parents in handling their child and in
> adjusting to her substantial handicap. The parents
> were very grateful for the elaborate medical
> interest that has been shown in the child." -
> Files: Assessment Unit.

But if doctors can record their approval of the way parents have taken information then it must be equally possible for them to make damaging judgements of the parents. But precisely because the doctors have little to offer, the parents may not find the information that they do receive very helpful. But the parents may not feel that they can express this criticism to the doctor concerned (see Stimson and Webb, 1975, p. 111), and without explaining to the doctor the reasons, may withdraw from the source of the information, namely the clinics. If the doctor then records his perception of events in the files this may then cast the parent in the role of trouble-maker - a moral judgement which cannot be challenged so long as the files are not open to the parents.

When medical knowledge is limited such that the diagnosis is not known, information about the nature of the child's disability is obviously recorded in files because without such records there would be no medical knowledge to speak of. But where there is a suspicion that the doctors' own procedures may be partly responsible for the child's condition, information will be withheld from parents as in these examples concerning the same child:

> "He will need to take Phenytoin for approximately two years after his last fit." - Files: Paediatrician.

> "One thing that is puzzling is the lack of growth in X's head over the past two years and the apparent slowing down of his developmental progress. I just wonder whether the latter may be due to Phenytoin toxicity." - Files: Doctor.

> "It is interesting, by the way, that since we have stopped giving Phenytoin his head circumference has started growing again." - Files: Doctor.

Professionals may worry that giving parents such information would make parents more anxious, but it would also increase their ability to judge the state of medical knowledge. It would reveal the extent to which medicine in these circumstances is a trial and error business for doctors (not to mention drug companies and their profits) and that their knowledge is far from one hundred per cent complete. To the extent that doctors hide their own uncertainties and the inadequacies of their procedures away from parents, this will make the parental expectation of complete medical knowledge that much more reasonable from the parents' point of view.

Even the issues surrounding the diagnosis itself spring from the limitations of medical knowledge. Because the parents are encouraged in their expectation of complete knowledge by the medical emphasis on diseases and cures, in a situation where there is no 'cure', the diagnosis becomes so important as to actually constitute medical knowledge and practice. It may be that when doctors do not have a known syndrome to work with they do not know how to listen to parents in the clinic because they do not have a yardstick against which to set the parents' comments, and that it is therefore easier for the doctors to put the comments down to parents' over-anxiety. But one must then ask in what way doctors think they are being helpful by holding a series of clinics which represent an extensive confirmation of the diagnosis and a monitoring of whether parents are reacting in the way in which doctors think they should. Sometimes, of course, a specific diagnosis is not known. Then the problems of giving the parents accurate and viable information are made more difficult when the doctors deceive themselves by creating complete new categories based on speculation or by making general statements seem more specific than they are:

> "AETIOLOGY: not well defined but probably minimal cerebral dysfunction." - Files: Assessment Unit.

> "AETIOLOGY: perinatal damage." - Files: Assessment Unit.

> "AETIOLOGY: developmental anomaly." - Files: Assessment Unit.

In addition, sometimes what passes for the medical diagnosis is a statement of the known physical outcome to various or unknown causes:

> "Cerebral palsy with spastic quadruplegia and microcephaly." - Files: Doctor.

> "Diagnosis: Hydrocephalus and Cerebral Palsy." - Files: Doctor.

> "Infantile convulsion associated with upper respiratory tract infection." - Files: Doctor.

Such physical outcomes will also create problems in respect of giving parents information about the diagnosis. As we have seen, without impressive-sounding syndromes to give as explanations, medical opinions (which are, unfortunately, sometimes presented as facts) about the child's future development may carry less authority with some parents. Indeed, children with epilepsy or cerebral palsy are not necessarily, not even usually, mentally-retarded, and there are many examples of intelligent physically-disabled children wrongly labelled mentally-retarded on such bases. However, there are other, equally damaging, outcomes arising from such uncertainties, namely professional speculations. The problem is that in seeming to fall short of cultural expectations in not being able to identify the cause of a disability, and striving to do so without letting parents know the extent of their uncertainty, can lead to the incorporation of socially-based judgements into the files as well as more strictly medical criteria. The best example of this is the logical muddle which occurs over the label 'educational subnormality' which is an educational-legal category, and which can be so all-embracing and subjective as to be meaningless (Tomlinson, 1982). In nearly half of the cases studied where there was a specific medical diagnosis lacking a senior clinical medical officer recorded 'educationally sub-normal' under the heading of diagnosis. Social judgements for which paediatricians and other hospital doctors have no valid training may emerge from attempts to derive a diagnosis through a blanket coverage of details, as in the following example.

> "Diagnosis: (1) Cerebral Dysfunction Syndrome
>   (2) Educationally Sub-Normal
>   (3) Speech Delay
>   (4) Enuresis
>   (5) Social Problem (divorced parents)"
>   - Files: Paediatrician.

From such social evaluations it is a small logical step to create even greater barriers to the parents receiving accurate information about the diagnosis (or lack of it) by incorporating social and administrative procedures into the professionals' considerations and decision-making.

> "It is appreciated that the boy has not yet been fully diagnosed, particularly with regard to his hearing. Nevertheless in view of his behaviour and retarded development I consider it correct for him to be admitted to (ESN(S) school) at the earliest opportunity." - Files: Medical officer.

(c) What Professionals Expect of the Parents

Doctors may expect that parents will not tell them everything they know or wonder about the child. Stimson and Webb (1975, pp. 43-44) point out that both doctor and patient are selective about what they tell each other and about what they listen to from each other. In such cases doctors may feel obliged to cover such possibilities by

giving parents some information just in case. It is clear
that doctors <u>can</u> give parents useful, appropriate and
sensitive information. Here a doctor explains to the
parents the reasons for not beginning drug therapy after
the child has had a convulsion:

DR	"That was a very brief kind of fit.
F	Yes.
DR	A short period only.
F	Yes.
DR	If it was a serious/twenty minutes or thirty minutes then I would start her on the treatment now myself.
M	I see, yes.
F	That's fair enough/
M	OK." - Paediatric clinic

However, not all unsolicited information is found useful by
the parents. For example in one paediatric clinic the
parents have to dutifully listen to a long account by the
doctor of how to obtain a dietary item they already have.
Or again, a doctor indulges in some lengthy nostalgia
about the development of services in the area. This in
turn may mean that parents will simply not listen to
everything being said to them. The doctors in their turn
may then feel they have to work to get the parents to
accept the professional viewpoint. But in such circumstances
giving information to the parents may in fact be
equivalent to imposing an unwanted, not to say
unwarranted, professional interpretation on them. It has
been demonstrated elsewhere how this may mean a doctor
misunderstands the nature of a practical problem (see
Chapter 3, p.67). But in holding certain misguided beliefs
(for example that a handicapped child means a
handicapped family) doctors may wrongly assume that
parents are waiting for professionals to raise such issues
as how a handicapped child affects siblings, with the
result that parents can be badgered into accepting the
professional perspective at a time when doctors may feel
they are being sympathetic and giving parents useful
information:

DR	"The fact that you will have a period without .... er X. And er/ and during that week, you know, you can give

> all your time probably to (sister).
>
> M   Yes, oh yes.
>
> DR   Because she does I am sure/Does she ever comment about what she can't do?
>
> M   She's very good. Oh, well/
>
> DR   You know, because of X.
>
> M   She's very good really.
>
> F   Yes.
>
> M   She's a very easy child.
>
> DR   Yes.
>
> M   I can just say: we can't go out today, it's raining, I can't take X.
>
> DR   Yes.
>
> M   She just accepts it.
>
> DR   She just accepts it.
>
> M   Whether she always will I don't know.
>
> DR   Well this is one of the things, you know ...... Some of the brothers and sisters get to the stage where: 'we can't do it because of .....'" - Visit by medical officer.

Another expectation that doctors seemingly have regarding parents of mentally-handicapped children is that the problem can be conceptualized in terms of how well the parents come to terms with the information and 'accept' (from the professional view) their child's handicap. In commenting on the reactions of parents in files which the parents themselves do not see, the doctors and other professionals are making moral judgements about them. Favourable comments are recorded when the general reaction of the parents is seen to be appropriate according to the professional view:

> "Since his mother is excellently adapted to the situation and other facilities as appropriate are being provided on a medical basis there doesn't seem any better arrangement which psychology or medicine could offer meantime." - Files: Educational Psychologist.

But this also means that there are implicit condemnations of those parents who are deemed not to have responded appropriately to the information given by the professionals.

> "Anti-convulsant medicine advised together with counselling to parents who are unable to accept the diagnosis and prognosis and are sacrificing the welfare of (two siblings) for X." - Files: Assessment Unit.

Such judgements of parents' reactions find their natural extension in the way that professionals, especially doctors, act as moral guardians of voluntary and state benefits. In this study a paediatrician had been the medical guarantor of an application to the Family Fund of the Rowntree Memorial Trust in the case of four of the parents. In circumstances where it is not clear which professionals should be responsible for informing parents of various voluntary and state benefits and where information is seemingly given on an ad hoc basis, it is clearly dangerous for professionals to distinguish between the moral worth of people to receive benefits, thereby maintaining a stigma for all. For in such circumstances it is at least a possibility that the best information will only be accorded to those deemed morally worthy, or at least not to be trouble-makers.

Certain other expectations of parents may lead to situations where professionals do not keep parents well-informed. As Stimson and Webb (1975, pp. 88 and 123-7) argue, doctors may expect that parents do not want the responsibility for decision-making. They may also be bored at what, for them, seem routine explanations. They may even feel that having to explain their procedures is tantamount to having to justify their actions. These are some possible explanations for a situation where in one quarter of the cases it is clear from the files that information is being exchanged between medical and psychological personnel, and indeed that decisions are being made on the basis of this information, without the parents even being aware that psychological services have begun to keep records on their children.

> "I enclose completed form SE-2 in respect of X. I have not seen him myself but from information supplied by (medical officer) would support his recommendation for admission to (ESN(S) school). Once he has begun attending there may be opportunities for Schools Psychological Service involvement." - Files: Educational Psychologist.

Part of this reluctance to keep parents fully informed may be the expectation that in explaining their actions professionals are not only increasing the ability of parents to judge what is going on, but also that this encourages them to demand their rights, an attitude that GPs have felt generally to be increasing (Cartwright, 1967, p. 57).

> "Mr. and Mrs. X are very anxious that X should have physiotherapy in order to enable him to walk unaided. Personally, I think that this is part of the general pattern of his retardation (...) I suspect that the parents distrust me and feel that I am keeping their child away from (school for physically-handicapped). If you could possibly find any glimmer of light to suggest that the boy might benefit academically from (school for physically-handicapped) I would go along with the physical need for his transfer." - Files: Medical officer writing to educational psychologist.

Presumably professionals find this demanding of rights regrettable not only because it shows up their discomfort and embarrassment, but because they fear the loss of their professional independence, and as part of this, that without parents' deference they cannot conduct the professional-client relationship in the old-fashioned spirit of gentlemanly patronage as they might wish.

Another occasion when parents may be given information is when parents are expected to do a considerable amount of work with their child. If professionals expect parents to do the work they have to get them to accept a professionals' perspective and this requires that they be given information. For example, in a lengthy conversation between an educational psychologist and a mother on the subject of a child's persistent incontinence, the psychologist begins by suggesting that the problem is one to do with the child's own motivation. He suggests that the mother should do some work in teaching the child to make its own bed, as well as teaching the child to keep its own chart of progress and instituting a system of rewards for keeping a dry bed. Information about child management is given because the mother is expected to do the work. Furthermore, it is interesting that suggestions for informing the parents that emerge from case-conferences seem to be connected to work expected of the parents, as mentioned in Chapter 3 (p. 53).

(d) How relationships between parents and professionals
     are managed
It has been argued that professionals may feel that giving parents explanations amounts to having to justify their actions. On the other hand it is on occasions when the routine relationships between professionals and parents are threatened that professionals may be prompted to give parents information precisely because the situation seems to require a justification. In this example a mother has been giving a medical officer information to keep him up to date about the hearing tests her child has had. She criticizes the attitude of some (unnamed) professionals and the medical officer produces a rationale. This is not to inform the mother (after all she has said as much to him) but to make sure he dissociates himself from the criticism and keeps relations on a good footing.

> M   "Because there was some suggestion, in some quarters, that X didn't hear because ·he didn't want to hear. And that is not so.
> DR   Well that/That's the reason for using the electrocochleography. To try and .... prove one way or the other which/
> M   Yes. Because it's very difficult." - Visit by medical officer.

Similarly, a clinic has become such a confusion of misunderstandings that only an explanation of why the paediatrician is asking the questions he is (not usually given) can save a total breakdown of the clinic:

> DR   "That's OK. What happened/I asked that question (about the) water infection. Because I saw these two (items in the file) continuously, see. So I thought that's where/she was having the water infection." - Paediatric clinic.

Of course the more information that professionals give parents the greater the ability of the parents to judge their decisions (Stimson and Webb, 1975, p. 134). With regard to doctors the issues of giving information also relates to the controversy as to whether the medical profession should be able to claim a monopoly on judging clinical competence. Such is the case in this situation where a paediatrician is giving the parents some information about a drug he is prescribing:

DR   "I should use the Dorbanex as necessary. (...)

F   If you give it her then does it break it up?

M   Does it soften the motion?

DR   Yes.

F   It's not er/

DR   The main function of Dorbanex is softening the stool. The sennapod/ See we divide laxatives in different classifications. They fall as er irritant laxative, bulk-forming laxative, cellulose/ increasing the vol/water content of the faeces.

M   Yes.

DR   These are the kinds of, er laxatives. The Dorbanex one is the/just softens the stool and nothing else, OK?" - Paediatric clinic.

Now clearly this drug cannot have a 'main function' (which suggests others, or another) and a single function as the final line suggests. In fact its classification as a stimulant laxative in the British National Formulary suggests a complex function if it is also a faecal softener. The information has been literally 'doctored' with the good intention, presumably, of reassuring the parents. Clinical control is thus another factor complicating the giving of information.

Stimson and Webb (1975, p. 111) suggest that patients are unwilling to make criticisms directly to the professional concerned. This in turn suggests that paediatricians will not know when parents would prefer to do without routine recalls to the clinic, or when parents do not find information about routine checks and procedures very helpful. Without a known diagnosis as well a doctor may only be able to offer help through the fact of the professional-client relationship itself. In such

157

circumstances doctors must fear that the relationship wears very thin when they have to give the parents the difficult information that they do not know the nature of the child's disability or how best to manage the child or how to find the appropriate service for the child. The uneasiness which threatens the ability of a doctor to manage professional-parent relationships shows itself in a number of ways. The doctor may transfer hope to establishing the information in the future:

DR   "And if you keep the appointment in May
M   In May.
DR   I hope by then I'll be able to sort of perhaps be able to tell you what I've found." - Paediatric clinic.

Or the doctor may offer a vague rationale about the use of medicine:

DR   "Really my contribution is really small now I fear, if there's anything. You know, it's a question of just sort of keeping a general medical eye on things." - Paediatric clinic.

The doctor's sense of unease may be such that it shows itself in the hesitancy of the speech used:

M   "I thought, oh, we've still got to get to the bottom of why he's like it.
DR   Right .... I think that's going to/quite honestly going to be ......
M   Mmn.
DR   That's going to be it
M   Yes I suppose it is.
DR   I don't think we're going to be able to give you a completely satisfactory answer." - Paediatric clinic.

As a final example, a doctor may transfer the emphasis in what is said from the nature of the child's disability (which is not known) to how to manage the child (which also may not be known by the doctor, but at least this transfers the focus to an area where the doctor knows the parents are receiving some kind of help).

> DR   "Well from the point of view of diagnosis, I/I don't know.
> M   No.
> DR   That there's much further to go really.
> M   No.
> DR   I mean a lot of people have seen him.
> M   Mmn.
> DR   And er we've all gone into extra details.
> (X   Bye-bye .... Hello-ooooooh!
> (DR   But really as far as that's concerned, of being able to describe the cause of X's problems (inaudible) But not any clues as to what the cause was.
> M   No.
> DR   And I think that's the way it perhaps will remain.
> M   Yes, yes.
> (DR   Um, so it's best now, I think, to concentrate on management.
> (X   Mummy. Bubb-ba. R-rrrrrrh!
> DR   And support and that sort of thing. So you feel that perhaps that's as well taken care of as you can at the moment?" - Paediatric clinic.

There can be little doubt that professionals expect parents to keep them well-informed. And if the experience of doctors is anything to go by, professionals also find that part of the difficulty of managing professional-client relationships is the idea that parents do not tell them everything they could (Stimson and Webb, 1975, pp. 43-4).

> T   "I felt that X's mother kept it from me (.....) She's never once mentioned about X having a teacher at home. When she started giving her that I don't know." - Educational case-conference.

This seems to confirm the idea as well that professionals think that control of information should be a matter for their discretion, used by them as a means for building up what they regard as good relationships. The problem lies in the fact that professionals may then decide not to keep parents informed on certain issues for the sake of managing their relationships with the parents, especially when they do not want to be the bringer of bad news. There were at least two occasions when the professionals confided in me as a researcher, without giving the parents the same information. In effect this placed me in a similar position to the professionals themselves. On reflection, I would indict myself as much as the professionals for not giving the parents the information. The pressures I felt were not wishing to upset the professionals or parents (making the continuation of the research easier) and being far from clear where the responsibility lay for giving parents the information. For example, here a doctor does not take an opportunity to explain why the supply of incontinence pads had been affected. Instead, he waits until the mother is out of the room before explaining to me as the researcher:

> DR   "Nappy rolls .... We'll look into that. It may well be mum's not here when they come. And we've found that if you leave them on the doorsteps in some places they disappear, so ..." - Visit by medical officer.

By informing the mother of this speculation to her face any misunderstandings could have been cleared up. In the second example, a mother is talking to a psychologist about various government allowances:

> M   "I didn't even know that I could get that attendance allowance until some mother told me here.
> (...)
>
> M   'Cause I'm trying to get'em free dinners. But I've got one form and I'm trying to claim/pointless having two forms. I might as well claim on the one form for the pair of them.
>
> EP   Aha, aha.
>
> M   And be done with it. So I'm filling that in at the moment.
>
> EP   I .... It's all/Yeh.
>
> M   I know we're both working but if you can

	get it, you might as well get it. I mean a lot of money's lost that way ain't it?
EP	Oh, yes. Sure. It's always worth having a try.
M	That's it, yeh.
EP	They'll tell you soon enough if they think you can't have it." - Meeting between Educational Psychologist and Mother.

Afterwards, the psychologist told me that not only would the mother not get free dinners for her children, but that the child's imminent transfer to an ESN(M) school would probably lose the attendance allowance as well, and he did not think that it was his responsibility to tell the mother himself (fieldwork diary). It seems that the professionals become so concerned with managing relationships that they forget the powerful position they are in with regard to the parents. The problem of information is not the apparent dilemma that professionals have of whether to give out certain information or not, but the fact that the professionals are involved in a power relationship such that the decision devolves to them. This is not to say, however, that professionals cannot manage power relations with sympathetic aims. Here a paediatrician does not give a mother all the information he might, presumably to spare her feelings at being informed that what she has been doing may have aggravated the problem:

DR	"The other thing is giving her antacids to neutralize the acid.
M	I've been giving her lemon juice and honey and all the acid things I could think of just to try and neutralize it.
DR	Well the best thing might be to try something like Milk of Magnesia or Alludrox. Alludrox gel or something like that." - Paediatric clinic.

But just as often the control of information may mean that the professionals feel they know the motivation of the parents and child (see Stimson and Webb, 1975, pp. 123-7). Consequently, they mistake damaging subjective evaluations of the parents for professional insight. Such 'insight-orientated' behaviour, discussed by Mayer and Timms (1970) in relation to social workers, may mean that various moral beliefs the professionals may hold do not constitute information to which the parents have access because such information might damage the management of relationships from the professional point of view.

> EP   "Both/because he's very high at home. I sometimes wonder if mother's concentration on these cognitive things is at the expense of, in order to avoid the question of control. I mean both children were performing badly for me, and didn't seem to respond very well when mum said, you know, stop it and slow down. Particularly the boy but X as well.
>
> T   And mum says that about X. I mean she's been in the classroom and seen X (inaudible) And she says, oh, she won't do a thing for me. You know, all in front of X. There's X listening." - Educational case-conference.

There is some indication that professionals feel that they should control the flow of information to the parents because of the possible reaction of parents to that information. Firstly, there is the feeling that parents will not understand the information:

> "Mrs. X appears to have misconstrued the comments of various professionals involved with X to suggest that there is now nothing holding his development back." - Files: Educational Psychologist.

There is also a suggestion that giving parents certain information will make them anxious. Taking into account the possibility that professionals do not understand that much themselves, and the likelihood that their explanations may have been brief and full of technical jargon, this is hardly surprising. But in the context of files unseen by the parents the comments of the professionals also constitute an implicit judgement of the parents. Some of the reluctance to give parents information may stem from the uncertainty which the professionals feel enters the relationship when the parents are given the type of information which could enable them to judge the performance of professionals:

> "His parents are puzzled and wonder if we all know quite what we are doing. They are particularly concerned that nobody is quite sure whether X can hear properly or not. The word 'autism' has made them wonder if he is at the right school." - Files: Doctor.

For doctors in particular, part of the concern of managing relations is the need to be sensitive, particularly when giving information to parents which is likely to distress them. Unfortunately, in trying to be sensitive the doctors may ignore entirely the gap between professional meaning and parental understanding. The doctors then mistakenly think that they have successfully explained the situation to the parents.

> "I have told her parents that she is slow at the moment but as yet it is too early to tell how she will develop. I have hinted strongly though that she could turn out to be abnormal." - Files: Doctor.

But sometimes such sensitivity appears to be part of a conscious management of professional relations with parents. Take the following two examples:

> "I have warned Mrs. X that it could be that in the second twelve months, X will not do quite as well as she did in the first. Even allowing for that though, I think X will do relatively well and especially so in view of the stimulation she is obviously getting at home." - Files: Paediatrician.

> "Obviously if we could improve his cardiac status he would be better off overall, though I have made it very clear to his parents that we will never be able to restore his mental and neurological status to normal." - Files: Doctor.

The first thing to note about the examples is that the information is dependent to a greater or lesser extent on opinion. Secondly, in both cases the doctor is starting from a situation where the parents are seen by the professionals to have 'accepted' the nature of the child's disability. And thirdly, in both cases the children have surprised the professionals with the progress they have made. This is confirmed by a variety of sources in both examples - files, fieldwork diary, educational review and interviews with parents. It seems that the information which doctors are presuming they have successfully conveyed is aiming to ensure that the progress does not lead the parents to review their expectations of their child, such that their adjustment to their child's disability does not become inappropriate from the doctor's point of view.

The feeling that the more parents know, the more they will be in a position to judge the professionals, can lead to very defensive attitudes to information-giving. So much so that when a context arises in which medical records of the child (which include many comments on the parents) are to be seen by a third party, the response of the doctors points to the very anti-democratic nature of keeping files in confidentiality from those who are commented upon:

> "As you will be aware this is a confidential document and the information received from the various professionals is sometimes fairly emotionally highly-charged. However, on looking through this I do not think that there is anything there which one would be anxious about the parents knowing, but I would ask you to protect us from any misunderstanding should this seem possible to arise." - Files: Doctor.

> "... I would carefully go through the reports to remove any contentious parts, as it is possible that the parents will get a sight of the reports themselves." - Files: Doctor.

Doctors may have their defensive attitudes further strengthened if they feel that the attitude of some parents is to demand their rights from professionals, as argued by Cartwright (1967, p. 57).

> "I listened to the parents' grumbles about the lack of contact from the various authorities but was able to remind them of my own letters to them of September 1978 and January of this year offering to see the parents when and where they

chose." - Files: Assessment Unit.

Such defensiveness, set in a context where the parents cannot reply to the right to reply as it were, constitutes a powerful evaluation of the parents. It is 'powerful' because the professionals can write the official history of events, unknown and unchallenged by the parents, and thus can effectively always have the final say in any disagreement. In fact a further danger in this instance occurs when events prove the professionals to be wrong. Then, there are no systematic means for deleting comments (written at earlier dates) which reflect badly on the parents, when perhaps part of the reason for the non-emergence of the relevant information was the professionals' protection of their own procedures and routines.

> "Mr. and Mrs. X are at present pursuing a claim for vaccine-damage although I feel there will not be any evidence to support this." - Files: Medical officer.

> "The problem at present is that the parents have applied for vaccine-damage payment and the history seems fairly compatible with this. One stumbling block seems to be the diagnosis of (name of syndrome)." - Files: Paediatrician.

The effect that relations between professionals have on information-giving is dealt with further in the next section.

(e) How relationships between professionals are managed
Even in cases where a professional is apparently taking time to give parents accurate and detailed information, problems still exist if one holds the view that information-giving should be a genuinely democratic sharing of knowledge. It has been suggested elsewhere that information arising out of assessments can have a variety of social functions (Dyson, 1987).
    As has been argued in the chapter on services, information about the services can be presented in such terms as to persuade the parents to use the services, irrespective of how appropriate the parents may feel that

165

the services are. But if the services are considered appropriate by the professionals, then the information may also contain a warning to liaise with the services in what the professionals consider to be the proper manner.

> DR "Um, if we're looking at somebody coming out 'to X and helping you with aspects of his development then it would be (medical officer) that would be recommending the service, OK?" - Paediatric clinic.

Part of this giving of information as a means of persuasion seems to have to do with the way in which professionals regard themselves as scarce resources. However, when information about the way in which services work is given to the parents, it seems that 'explanations' draw on such ideas as if they were part of a stock of professional rhetoric. Moreover, it is done in such a way as to effectively evaluate the parents as troublesome:

> "Parents were rather resentful to attend the outpatient clinic frequently so I gave them the usual explanation that X will need team work, and this is the best way of allocating resources." - Files: Doctor.

Another aspect of such information-as-persuasion may be related to the fear of losing professional independence and professional control over working conditions, a fear identified by Cartwright and Anderson (1981, p. 75). To the extent that professionals feel that relationships between them are managed through bureaucracies on behalf of the state, they are likely to have a conservative attitude to information-giving. They may find the routine nature of some of their work boring, including informing the parents if they perceive it to be superfluous and the cause of much administrative work. This appears to be the reason that information-giving is mocked in this example, where the reference is to a standardized letter from the County Education Officer, sent whenever a child is to change school.

> EP "And the (ESN(M) school) thing we'll get

> going. And I dare say you'll have one of
> those little typed letters from ...
> (M   I suppose I shall (inaudible).
> (EP   The usual thing. Exactly the same words
> as you got for his brother." - Meeting
> between Educational Psychologist and
> Mother.

However, when it comes to being kept informed themselves, the professionals are more likely to see the advantages of routinized networks of information, as they admit themselves:

> "None of the usual paperwork appears to have been done (usually a cause for celebration) but in this instance it has meant that (the home tutor) has been plugging away with X without my ever having been informed that she had even been appointed." - Files: Educational Psychologist.

It would seem that professionals expect to be kept informed themselves, either about the management of the child or about the other services involved. To my mind, the following comment by a professional could equally well be the sort of comment a mother might wish to make about professionals who are not keeping her informed about her child, and seems to offer a good justification of why professionals should have a duty to keep parents well-informed.

> "To save duplication of effort and avoid clashes of aims or techniques, it would be very helpful if you could let me have any details of what the X's are doing with X." - Files: Educational Psychologist.

CONCLUSION

It has been argued in this chapter that there are a variety of reasons why information is not the resource it could be for parents of mentally-handicapped children.

Because of the many social and political dimensions to any information, giving parents accurate information is a starting point, not an end in itself. It is when professionals assume that their information is purely factual that they tend to label the child or be insensitive. Not all parents hold the medical view that the social nature of the problems is to fill in gaps in medical knowledge through research. But many doctors do, and beyond trying to establish the diagnosis they are uncertain what they can do except to be sympathetic and report any problems in their files. Sometimes the information professionals give to try and fill this space is found to be unhelpful, and sometimes lack of medical knowledge about the workings of drug therapies is not communicated to the parents. To the extent that psychologists have a clinical, hospital-based perspective, the work that parents do towards child management at home may be used as a rationale for not being able to help the parents with such management problems themselves. When the diagnosis of a syndrome or condition is relatively straightforward, the problem of information associated with diagnosis will be in distinguishing the necessary, as opposed to the socially determined outcomes of a disability. Confusing the two will limit the child unnecessarily.

The problem of parents receiving adequate information from professionals is in some senses a problem misconceived, since the parents (and parents' groups) are the real experts on their own children. Sometimes, therefore, information from professionals is little more than a restatement of the mother's own words. The limitations to medical knowledge mean that doctors may emphasize routine measurements or blood tests. Some parents are reassured by such thoroughness, others are irritated and inconvenienced. Doctors continue to command clinical control and social privilege when the orientation of medicine in this instance is limited to specific physical problems when the child is very young. To the extent that doctors hide their own uncertainties and the inadequacies of their procedures (e.g. that some drug therapies are little more than trial and error) away from parents, parents will continue to expect 100% knowledge from doctors. Because there is no cure, diagnosis is primarily what constitutes medical knowledge in this area. But in trying to make their information authoritative, doctors are sometimes too quick to associate epilepsy, cerebral palsy or multiple physical disabilities with mental handicap. Or they even incorporate non-medical judgements into the diagnosis (e.g. 'ESN' or 'divorced parents').

Because doctors may expect that parents will not tell them everything, doctors may give some information 'just in case'. At best this unasked-for information can be useful and sensitive. At worst it is an imposition of an unwarranted professional perspective on the situation. One example is the idea that a handicapped child equals a handicapped family. Another is that the problem can be expressed in terms of how well parents 'accept' the professional view of their child's handicap. This can lead to some highly evaluative judgements being written in professional files where they cannot be challenged. Professionals may also become so involved in their own routines that they omit to keep parents informed about what is happening.

Sometimes information is used almost as a conciliatory measure when relations between professionals and parents threatens to break down, and sometimes it is prompted by the fact that the mother is required to do the corresponding work. The medical claim to clinical control also complicates matters since the more information that professionals give parents, the greater the ability of the parents to judge their decisions. The uneasiness which doctors feel when they have little or no relevant information to give parents occurs because without a known diagnosis, doctors may concentrate on making the best of the professional-client relationship. The uneasiness is because without information to give parents the relationship is largely without substance and thus largely without relevance. Professionals do, however, expect parents to keep them informed in a variety of ways. But often they become so concerned with managing relationships, they forget their powerful position with regard to the parents, and avoid taking responsibility for giving parents relevant information. In some situations they are so concerned whether or not to give parents information that they forget the very problem is that they are in a powerful position such that the decision devolves to them. Sometimes this power is used sensitively, but when the professionals feel they have a privileged insight, this often results in moral evaluations of parents and child. Some professionals may feel that they should not give parents certain information because they would not understand it and it would make them anxious. But this is hardly a justification if explanations are given in technical jargon. If professionals try to communicate information sensitively by hinting, the result may be that the information is neither received nor understood. If professionals feel that increasing the knowledge of the parents will enable them to better judge the professionals, then the professionals will be very defensive about letting parents have such information. So much so that where professionals write the 'official' records of events in files this will constitute a powerful evaluation of the parents.

However, giving parents accurate information is not just dependent on the goodwill of professionals. Information may take as given certain social arrangements which historically have developed in a specific way and which in principle can be changed. Or alternatives which may be suggested only fall within a very narrow political range. Or information may be a social artefact of certain professional routines and relationships which are not therefore 'natural' and not therefore necessary. Furthermore, information may be given to persuade parents to use professional services which are regarded as scarce resources. Professionals dislike having to convey bureaucratic and routine information, but dislike it even more if such routines break down and they are not informed themselves such that they cannot do their jobs. This suggests that professionals should have a duty to convey clear and accurate information to parents so that the parents can best perform the work they do with their children.

It has been argued that information should be a resource that could be used by parents and children in order to give them greater control over their own lives. At the very least this would require files and case-conferences to be completely open to the parents. The problem of other information stems from the fact that it is generated in the context of an unequal relationship, where the way in which parents relate to the professionals is examined and judged. Information generated on the basis of mutually segregated experiences will not, largely, create a resource for parents of mentally-handicapped children to tackle the problems with which they are faced on their own terms and in ways which are under their own control.

Chapter Six

AN OPEN LETTER TO PARENTS OF MENTALLY-
HANDICAPPED CHILDREN

(a) Introduction
As it is being suggested that parents of handicapped
children need control over the solutions to their own
problems, and that parents' groups can help, then where
does all this lead us? In 1982 it led a group of parents in
the West Midlands (Family Focus, 1982) to write a
pamphlet addressed to the professionals. In it they argued
that the assessment of children with special needs should
be more of a partnership between parents and professionals,
and that also the child should be included in this
partnership. They also pointed out that the parents need
to understand the roles and the procedures of the
professionals. This would also help parents to judge the
relevance of the various services. They argued as well
that the parents need to know what professionals think of
their child (which would mean access to files and
case-conferences), and that the professionals need to take
notice of information parents give them. If these are
likely to be the aims of parents' groups, we must also
consider the difficulties such groups may face.

(b) A Partnership between Professionals and Parents?
It is important to remember that any partnership between
professionals and parents is unlikely to be equal, given
that the professionals have more material resources than
most parents, greater status, and control access to the
services they provide. Self-help groups of parents are
important in redressing the unequal balance to some
extent. They do this by creating a pool of knowledge

171

which parents can draw upon. They may also reduce the sense of abandonment and isolation that parents might otherwise feel. In the long term, however, any challenge to the authority of the professionals will be weakened by the feeling that ultimately parents have to rely on those professionals. "We try to keep in with people at the hospital because you never know when you'll need them", or "you daren't make too much of a fuss for the child's sake", or "they're not very useful but who else have we got?" are typical of the worries that parents have. But because many different professionals are involved in dealing with a handicapped child parents may try to turn to the professional who they personally find most supportive. But this will make it seem that the problem is to do with personalities of some other professionals, rather than to do with the power that professionals have in general.

However, there are problems even in trying to establish more equal relations with professionals by asking for more co-operative and good relationships. As we have already seen professionals sometimes do not criticize one another in order to maintain 'good relationships'. It seems possible that an obsession with parents and professionals 'getting on' could drastically reduce the chances of getting the best deal for the child. What this means, I think, is that the child may best be helped by the parents questioning professional judgements, challenging the right of professionals to use certain procedures and resisting the attempts of professionals to define their problems for them. This can be done, as comments from the parents themselves illustrate:

> "You asked me before what sort of advice we would give to other parents. And what we have always said to sum all this up is the fact that we always question everything. To question anything that's ever told them. Um, to get a second opinion. Question, go really into, never accept the first (...) report. No. Never, never, never."

(c) Politics and Choices
Involving the child in the partnership to help decide on issues that will affect his or her life seems possible for those who are physically disabled or moderately handi-

capped. However, if we look at what this means in the case of a child who is severely mentally-handicapped, then allowing the child some choice in its own life seems difficult. This idea of choice also seems part of a wider concern for the handicapped to be treated as proper human beings. The problem is that as soon as the ability to choose becomes a necessary part of what we think it means to be human, the logical outcome is that those who apparently cannot exercise the skill of choosing (i.e. the very severely mentally-handicapped) are degraded. Of course parents of the so-called 'severely mentally-handicapped' will recognize ways in which their child can choose. But, firstly, this view may not be shared by professionals or by society at large. And, secondly, the range of choices may be artificially imposed from above (e.g. which of two cakes a child would like to eat) and therefore other options may be excluded. This second point has similarities to the way political choice works in our own democracy, as I will attempt to argue below. Meanwhile, some people may point out that improvement in communication skills and technology (e.g. talking-machines operated by touching keyboards) will enable increasing numbers of people with disabilities to make choices for themselves (especially some of those with cerebral palsy). But the result would be that such people would no longer be seen as mentally handicapped, but physically disabled, that what is presented as a choice between integration and segregation is always resolved in favour of segregation. The issue of giving mentally-handicapped children choices raises a number of political dilemmas. These are summarized below. A more detailed discussion of politics and choices follows in the final chapter.

1. Requests that a disabled child be included in a partnership of decision-making implies that making choices is part of what it means to participate fully in our society. The danger of such requests is that they continue to exclude those of the severely mentally-handicapped who apparently cannot choose.
2. In a democracy political control is achieved by presenting the public with ready-made, limited choices. The issue of how best to educate children with disabilities is presented as segregation versus integration. Other fundamental questions about what kind of provision we want for all children are never raised.

3. Furthermore, precisely because the type of provision made for so-called 'normal' children is taken for granted, then the segregation versus integration issue is always, will always be, effectively resolved in favour of segregation. This is because 'normal' provision is based on timetables, getting through syllabuses in a certain limited amount of time and is seen to require the exclusion of those who would disrupt the routine, which includes the 'maladjusted', 'slow learners' as well as the disabled and the mentally handicapped.

4. The Conservative Government's policy is a good example of how the aims of the education system are hidden and not subject to open debate, as the language of legislation and White Papers shows. Firstly, separate parts of government documents argue for the freedom of the child, or the freedom of the parents. However, the freedom of either depends on the restriction of the other. Therefore the _real_ choice of parents' versus child's freedom is not even acknowledged let alone resolved. Secondly, the democratic decision-making over a child's schooling includes different people according to which parts of the official documents one reads. The conflict of interests that is not being faced here is parents of handicapped children versus the taxpayer. In the official documents the interests of the taxpayer take preference, presumably because there are more other types of taxpayer to vote than parents of handicapped children. But this is not a case of a democratic majority decision, for similar arguments can be made for many parallel spheres of life, where disadvantaged groups (women, unemployed, poor, physically disabled, elderly, ethnic minorities) are denied a full participation in society. These groups are defeated individually when together they would form the majority. Thirdly, the duties of local authorities are apparent not real, though they appear real because of clever wording. Furthermore, the only alternative to segregation is thought to be holding back the intellectual development of the 'normal' child. And yet we are supposed to believe that this opposition of interests between the mentally handicapped and other children can disappear when these other children grow up and become professionals! Finally, again on the subject of the interests of the taxpayer, it needs to be noted that this will not include mothers of handicapped children who are not paid a wage in the first place for the work that they do.

5. The suggestion that disabled children be included in the decision-making partnership seems to spring from such values as humanity, democracy, freedom and equality. The weakness of such a good suggestion is that it is made within the constraints of a society where such values have little meaning in practice.

(d) Understanding what the professionals do

It is certainly true that parents need to understand the roles and the procedures of the professionals, but what professionals write in explanatory pamphlets or otherwise state by way of explanation is not what actually occurs. It seems unlikely that professionals would be enthusiastic about defining their own procedures because the parents would then have a reference point from which to challenge them. This may be deduced from situations where procedures are defined, such as in legislation. For example, the 1981 Education Act is said to give the parents the right of appeal in the question of schools provision, supposedly right up to the level of Secretary of State. But there are a great many practical difficulties in the way of the effective working of such a procedure, as a reading of sections 7-16 of the 1981 Education Act shows. The following represented on anticipation of how the procedures laid down might not work in practice:

(i) Having assessed the child, the local education authority (LEA) sends the parents a copy of the statement of the child's special educational needs. However, there may be some parents who do not understand the wording of the document, especially if it is written in jargon (section 7(3)).

(ii) Although the parents must also be notified about their right to make representations to the authority about the statement and/or to require a meeting with an officer of that authority within the 15 days specified, understanding the statement itself does not necessarily mean that the parents will understand the implications of the statement for the type of schooling their child will receive (sections 7(4) and 7(7)).

(iii) If the parents disagree with the assessment they can require the LEA to arrange further meetings (although the persons required to be at such meetings are decided on by the LEA not by the parents). However, whether it is practical or possible for a mother to get to such a meeting (because of the problem of transport or having other children to look after) is another matter. Nor is it clear just how many "further meetings" the parents can require. In any case the expense of travel and/or taking time off work then becomes a factor (section 7(5)).

(iv) The LEA can then confirm, modify or retract the statement, inform the parents of this, and of their right to appeal, and of the name of the person to whom they have the right to appeal (section 7(8)).

(v) The parents may then, provided of course that they have the determination to keep resisting the LEA's decision, appeal to an appeals committee (established in accordance with the 1980 Education Act) (sections 8(1) and 8(2)).

(vi) The appeals committee can confirm the LEA's decision, or they can ask the LEA to reconsider, though this is not binding on the LEA (section 8(4)).

(vii) In either case the parents can appeal in writing to the Secretary of State, which in itself requires a certain amount of practical know-how on the part of the parents (sections 8(5) and 8(6)).

(viii) The Secretary of State can confirm or amend the statement, or else direct the LEA to stop keeping a statement on that child (section 8(7)).

(ix) If, however, during or after the above procedure the LEA decides to serve a school attendance order on the parents, then the parents are given the opportunity to decide which school should be named in the order, which of course requires knowledge about the schools locally (section 15(2)).

(x) The LEA can, however, ask the Secretary of State to name a different school from that the parents wish (section 15(4)).

(xi) While the order is in force the parents can apply to have the school named in the order changed or to make their own educational arrangements (e.g. home tuition) which the LEA can simply ignore by claiming that the other school is unsuitable, that resources would not then be used efficiently, or that the parents' own arrangements are unsatisfactory (section 16(2)).

(xii) If the parents have any energy left they can make another appeal to the Secretary of State who finally decides (section 16(3)).

In order to make the most of their rights in this matter it can be seen that the parents need to be well-informed; not intimidated by professionals or authority; not subject to practical difficulties or pressures; and to have time, money, transport, and the sheer mental and physical energy to deal with such procedures. Many of these factors are, however, the very troubles which affect the parents of a child with disabilities the most. Moreover, these factors all reduce the chances of the defined procedures of legislation acting as a control on the power of the professionals to act as they see fit in any given situation. The procedures can even serve to maintain the control and power that the professionals have. This is because the procedures are <u>PROSPECTIVE:</u> they refer to what could happen in the future. Thus the professionals are in a position to argue along the lines of 'we could issue an attendance order but what we are more concerned about is the child's best interests' or 'you could appeal but the committee is bound by law to make a judgement in terms of special educational need' in both cases trying to create for the parents the image that they are the ones who are being unreasonable. In the end it seems plausible that the professionals could use the procedures in such a way as to discourage the parents from ever using them. So much for nationally-defined procedures. As for locally-produced or personal explanations of the procedures of professionals, these too will not be a fair reflection of what actually takes place. This is because the procedures are <u>RETROSPECTIVE:</u> they refer back to what has already taken place. That is, a decision based on administrative considerations may be presented to the parents as an educational decision. Or a decision that has already been made without consulting parents may be presented as an educational decision with parents consulted. For example, in this study it might be claimed that the role of medical officers is to assess children with special needs in order to decide what was the most appropriate form of schooling for them. However, their real role may often be to persuade parents of a decision that has already been made, as illustrated in Chapter 4, p. 117. In fact, out of the twenty parents whose children attend the ESN(S) school, only twelve claimed that their children had been seen by the Senior Clinical Medical Officer <u>before</u> they started at the school part-time. That administrative concerns are at the back of this doctor's mind may be deduced from a comment made to the headmistress of the ESN(S) school who had remarked on the falling number of children being admitted to the school: 'Don't worry I'm sure we'll always find a use for your school' (fieldwork diary). Similarly, what in terms of claimed procedures would be the involvement of the educational psychologist in assessment and school placement is in fact merely the rubber-stamping of a decision that has already been made, as demonstrated in Chapter 5, p. 154. This, in my sample, was the rule rather than the exception - none of the group of twenty children had been seen by a psychologist before they started school.

Many parents are obviously aware that what professionals claim to do is at best an idealized version of what happens and at worst amounts to straightforward evasion. However, persuading the professionals to define their roles and explain their procedures is only a useful exercise if the professionals can be held to account when they are inconsistent or break their own rules.

(e) Files and Case-Conferences

It is certainly true that parents need to know what the professionals think of their child. What the professionals really think of a child (and indeed its parents) is contained in professionals' files and in what is said at case-conferences. But medical, psychological and educational files contain social judgements; evaluations of the parents' moral worth; impressions; half-truths and unsubstantiated rumour. It is, therefore, easy to see why professionals would not want parents to see the files. The primary function of files is, of course, the protection of professionals, as this quotation shows:

> "I listened to the parents' grumbles about the lack of contact from the various authorities but was able to remind them of my own letters to them (...) offering to see the parents when and where they chose." - Files: Doctor.

They provide a reference point from which professionals can counter any accusations that they have not fulfilled their responsibilities correctly.

If required on the grounds of civil liberties to reveal

the contents of their files, there are several strategies available to the professionals:

(i) To 'clean out' any sensitive parts of the records. (see p. 164).

(ii) Hiding the files (Schrag and Divoky, 1981, p. 193).

(iii) Refusing to classify as files data they did not wish the parents to see or control (Schrag and Divoky, 1981, p. 193).

(iv) A generally obstructive attitude:

> "The parents had to make an appointment weeks in advance and they would then be shown the file or portions of the file, in the presence of an assistant principal or other school official. The parents were not permitted to take notes, make copies, or in many cases even to hold anything in their hands. The results would be 'interpreted' for them by the official." (Schrag and Divoky, 1981, p. 195).

(v) Privatization of files:

> "'If there was ever a requirement to give parents access to those records', said one (teacher), 'I'd keep them at home, bring in only those I need each day, and insist that they're my private files which don't belong to the school.'" (Schrag and Divoky, 1981, p. 196).

(vi) The professionals denying that they have the authority to release the files to the parents.

In effect, an indication of how great a distance has been created between parents, and what may be regarded as their right to know what professionals really think about them and their child can be taken from the same parents' reactions to my apology when I realized that I had seen files without first asking their permission (see Chapter 2, pp. 14-15). Given these reactions, many parents would find nothing unusual in a professional denying that he/she has the authority to release the file to the parents.

(vii) <u>Files written in idiosyncratic shorthand, hieroglyphics or jargon.</u>

Jargon, or professional terminology, is currently used as a reason not to reveal the contents of files "because the parents wouldn't understand" and it seems reasonable to assume that, if the files were to be made open, anything that could be more obscurely expressed would be. Thus even in a rare example of doctors allowing patients access to their files (an antenatal clinic in Portsmouth), the doctors developed ways of controlling information:

> "The use of marks and symbols on the records to indicate matters the doctors do not necessarily wish to tell their patients about is of great interest. So far as the doctors are concerned this is being done for the protection of the patient but they have not enquired from their patients to what extent they wish to be protected." (Cohen, 1982, p. 27)

However, let us suppose that this struggle by parents for access to their children's files has been won. I have no doubts that the parents would wish to challenge the professionals over some of the social judgements that are typically recorded in the files. For example, would parents be prepared to allow any of the following judgements to remain on record?

(i)   "The whole family is a social problem." - Files: Doctor
(ii) " ... immature parents ..." - Files: Doctor.
(iii) "Father (...) rather old appearance (...) rather a shy anxious man" - Files: Assessment Unit.

Indeed, most files contain an implicit evaluation of the parents by the professionals, an evaluation based on the degree to which parents react to circumstances as the professionals think they should, and on the extent to which these reactions cause problems for the professionals. Between 'problem families' and 'happy, united families' at the extremes there are even judgements about the way parents should present their actions:

"The parents provide very good care but I wish they could relax a little and enjoy the care of X." - Files: Assessment Unit.

However, it is interesting to note that one of the first consequences of open files (that is, where clients have free access to what professionals have written about them) is that the professionals are more careful and considerate in what they write:

"The consequences of the open record system for the doctors in the hospital have been interesting. They have found that they have to think carefully before writing comments in the patient-held records. Whereas before a doctor may have written 'silly bitch' on the patient's records she or he now finds that the situation has to be discussed with a patient (...) Because they know the patient will read the notes the doctors are also more careful about recording medical information. For example, rather than asking for a test to query an abnormality it can be requested to exclude an abnormality. The doctors feel that on balance it does not prejudice the patient that they sometimes cannot write things in the notes." (Cohen, 1982, p. 24).

"So far as people outside the centre are concerned, knowing that their reports will be read by the subjects of them means that they have to consider the impact of what they are writing. Throwaway remarks put down unthinkingly can take on the appearance of fact after a passage of time." (Cohen, 1982, p. 31)

A good example illustrating this last quotation is the way in which a doctor's observation or opinion that, at a particular moment in time, a mother is concerned about her child takes on the status of a neurosis when comments like 'X is an anxious mother' are written in the child's file, and remain on file to be read years later.

However, the social and contestable information contained in files does not end at this uncompilicated level. For example, the socially-constructed 'Educational Sub-Normality' (a legal-educational term) is used by the medical profession as if it were a medical syndrome. But 'ESN' means everything and nothing:

> " ... a child could be educationally backward with a high or low IQ; he or she could be ESN without requiring special schooling, or could be of above average ability and still require special schooling." (Tomlinson, 1982, p. 63).

There is another drawback to complaints about files kept on children which appeal to civil rights and liberties. This concerns the 'casework' approach that is the basis of medical, educational and psychological as well as social work records. Even if the files are 'open' the parents will only have access to one file, namely that of their own child. Consider, however, the following extract from the file of a child labelled ESN(Severe):

> "I suspect that the parents distrust me and feel that I am keeping their child away from (school for physically handicapped children with an IQ level of 50 or above). If you could possibly find any glimmer of light to suggest that the boy would benefit academically from (this) school, I would go along with the physical need for his transfer." - Files: Medical Officer.

So do the services operate a strictly educational criterion for admission to special schools? Not at all, as the following extracts from different case studies demonstrates:

> "I have not seen the boy myself but would support the (Senior Clinical Medical Officer's) recommendation that he be admitted to the special care unit attached to (the ESN(S) school), the length of attendance per week to be negotiated between the unit and the parents, the aim being largely parental relief." - Files: Educational Psychologist.

> "The (Senior Clinical Medical Officer) thinks it (admission) is <u>best</u> a) for a break for mum, b) some social contact, c) not a great deal educationally." - Files: Educational Psychologist.

> "Initially I had hoped that he would be able to at least attempt the local primary school, but, due to his lack of toilet training this proved to be impracticable. X was admitted to the ESN(S) school." - Files: Medical Officer.

In addition, various other reasons were presented to parents in the East Midlands for continued educational placement of their children in the ESN(S) school. One Down's child was not considered for transfer to an ESN(M) school because, although relatively bright, he was still 'borderline for this area'. A girl was not transferred because the ESN(M) school was said not to have a 'language-based curriculum'. Another girl was not moved to the school for the physically handicapped because 'her mental handicap is worse than her physical one.' In other words educational need, parental relief, social stimulation, administrative convenience, practical convenience, type of curriculum, state of handicap, as well as performance on developmental tests are used as justifications for school placement as and when the professionals see fit, even when they think they are trying to 'work the system' for the benefit of the child. Parents, who could only have access to one file (that of their own child) have no means to challenge the immense licence of power the professionals have, because the professionals can use different arguments to justify each specific case decision, and the fact that these decisions contradict one another, or are inconsistent, is hidden from the parents. What professionals really think of one child can only be understood in relation to what they really think of other children.

As far as case-conferences are concerned, my experience is that the professionals already have a stock of answers with which to justify the continued exclusion of parents:

(i) 'Parents will not understand what is said'. Once again, there is no professional terminology that could not be explained in straightforward language. The problem with simple language is that it is more easily challenged as the following example demonstrates. An eminent professor told parents that their child had a certain rare syndrome on the basis of an examination lasting five minutes. The parents asked him what this was. 'You wouldn't understand our medical terms,' he replied. The parents asked if there was a book they could consult on the matter only to be told that there was no such book written on the subject. Discovering a book by accident months later they compared their daughter with the description and photographs in the book and on this basis challenged the diagnosis, eventually winning a legal claim for compensation.

(ii) 'Professionals would not feel able to float ideas for discussion, put forward half-baked ideas, hunches etc.' This suggests that the way professionals produce knowledge about a client involves the exclusion of parents as well as the child. However, the net effect is that professionals will make judgements outside their own discipline, which because of their origin in a multi-disciplinary setting acquire the gloss of respectability. Judgements about parents' psychological character, social adaquacy, intellect or moral standing can be made by people who have no training to make such judgements.

(iii) 'Parents who know too much will worry unnecessarily' But parents will be worried anyway by the need for a case-conference and by not knowing what is being said. What the professionals are worried about is being seen to be uncertain or indecisive, thus creating a poor impression. This point seems to have similarities to research that has been done on doctors' clinics which suggests that problems in communication stem from the doctors hiding their own uncertainty (and thereby increasing that of their patients) as a means of retaining professional power (Waitzkin and Stoeckle, 1972, quoted and confirmed in Stacey, 1980).

(iv) 'Any professional, having given the most minimal contribution can cross-examine the parents and ask the most personal and revealing questions of them' Having heard a doctor use this argument, I suspect that this represents a medical intolerance of what are regarded as 'lesser' professionals. Of course, the problem could easily be overcome by including in the case-conference a friend/representative/guarantor. But what remains to be said about 'service' professionals whose clients need to protect themselves from abuse of privilege at any meeting?

(v) 'Some people argue for the inclusion of parents just to make a (political) point rather than considering the

best interests of the child' The political point that I
believe the professionals are worried about is the idea
that they should be accountable for their statements and
actions, not just to their respective professional bodies but
to the general public and particularly to the clients
themselves. I believe that the professionals can no longer
claim to be worthy of self-regulation, on account of the
inconsiderate way in which their files have come to
include personal value-judgements, not distinguished as
such from other material in the files, and not subject to
checking by those about whom they are written. However,
some professionals apparently cannot conceive of the idea
of full participation by the parents in case-conferences
simply because for them a key component to the very idea
of a case-conference involves the exclusion of the client.
Professionals want to provide good services but they want
to do so on their own terms and on condition that the
clients respond in what the professionals regard as an
appropriate way. This is what underlies the 'contract' that
some service professionals speak of offering the clients.
But what, in effect, should be the subject of open public
debate (how parents of a child with special needs and that
child can best be helped - therefore a political issue) is
defined by professionals as outside politics, and is reduced
to an apparently 'natural' course of events. The question
becomes one of how much of which service, not what type
of service is appropriate and why. The whole basis by
which professionals relate to clients is then hidden, and
the unequal power relationship that it involves is denied.
Anyone who then argues that parents have a right to
attend the whole of a case-conference is accused of being
political. But it is equally political to deny that there is a
political issue at stake, and to appeal to 'the best
interests of the child' is merely an attempt to consolidate
the false presentation of the exclusion of parents from
case-conferences as a natural and logical occurrence.
There is no reason why making a valid political point, and
fighting to see that point implemented, should not also be
in the best interests of the child.

(f)   How information is used by professionals
Professionals certainly need information from parents, but
they also in practice use it selectively and for their own
purpose. For example, the medical officers may, when

1 85

assessing a child, ignore or play down what the parents claim the child can do in favour of their own immediate observations. However, when the assessment proves impractical in some way, then the entire assessment may be based on questioning the parents.

Research in paediatric clinics has shown that doctors need information from parents in various ways, and for a variety of reasons. Firstly, the doctors select information from the explanation given in the parents' own terms in order to arrive at what they consider to be the medically relevant details (Davis, A., 1982, p. 114). Secondly, information given by parents to doctors is taken up by the doctors and used against the parents to judge their credibility. The doctors use medical records and referral letters as a means to check the validity of what the parents are saying. Indeed, as with the medical officer, the doctors only seem to turn to the parents for information when their preferred sources are blocked for whatever reason:

> "As often happened, the child either performed the tests in a desultory fashion, did not perform at all, or was so disruptive that the physical examination was curtailed, the doctor became completely dependent on the parents' replies. As well as assessing the child he had to assess the credibility of the parents." (Davis, A., 1982, p. 114).

Thus doctors in the clinics are asking parents for information about their child, and then to some extent using that information for a different purpose from that for which it was given, namely to judge the credibility of the parents:

> "A key aspect of this was the extent to which parents talked about their child as data, as detached observers who reported reliably on the child's failures as well as successes. An anxious over-involvement with the child was taken as a sign that the mother's account was biased in the child's favour." (Davis, A., 1982, p. 115).

Thirdly, it is interesting to note which parents the doctors actually credit with a degree of expertise. It is not necessarily those mothers, for example, whose past or present employment as a nurse, health visitor, therapist or teacher gives them a body of knowledge, whom the doctors credit with some expertise, but rather those who have attended the clinic on a regular basis, and have allowed themselves to be 'trained' to be 'ideal observers' from the doctor's point of view (Davis, A., 1982, pp. 117-20). This brings us to the fourth point which is that parents are variously rewarded by the doctors depending on their outlook, and therefore the information which they gave to the doctor.

> "The parents who adjusted expectations were regarded as 'good parents', the ones who did not became the subject of case-conferences or social work intervention." (Davis, A., 1982, p. 131)

Indeed, in the East Midlands study, the professionals had in some cases successfully encouraged the parents to present information in the terms the professionals themselves used. Parents talked of their child 'having problems with fine movement'; 'having autistic traits'; 'being hyperactive' or 'needing behaviour modification'. This degradation of their own viewpoint by some of the parents will be 'rewarded' by statements in the professional files to the effect that 'Mother has fully accepted X's handicap'. Finally, doctors in clinics also need information from parents for their own purposes in two related ways. In the first place doctors want the parents to put forward the information rather than continually asking the parents questions:

> "Since the doctor had very little to offer the parents, to make his interrogative tactics too overt would be to threaten the parents' co-operation and even attendance at the clinic." (Davis, A., 1982, p. 120)

And secondly, information from parents is a way of filling up the time of the clinic when the doctor has very little to offer, perhaps when the child is already at school:

> "The time was filled in with the routine testing, a few questions about other services, and the doctor flicking through the case notes in search

of new topics of conversation or things to check. Some parents, therefore, particularly working-class ones seem to define repeated visits as a waste of time and ceased coming." (Davis, A., 1982, p. 136)

Whilst it is true that professionals need information from parents, a way needs to be found of ensuring that professionals give credit to parental information on its own terms, and do not merely use it to judge and categorize the parents, or indeed use the information for their own purpose only.

(g) Conclusion

It should be clear from what has been written that part of the weakness of parents' groups is the need to bring about quite broad political change before they can have more say in dealing with their own children's problems. Now, although every child is an individual in its own right, and creates, in certain respects, very individual needs for the parents, there are many issues both have in common with other parents and children, handicapped, or otherwise. And it is only by finding common ground with other groups that parents' groups will develop:

(i) new ideas for coping with practical problems,

(ii) new strategies for dealing with services,

(iii) sufficient numbers to form pressure groups, pool resources and gain enough power to get things changed.

The extent of the problem to be faced can be seen by the fact that the strategies that seem most likely to bring results are the very strategies that are most difficult to implement, and which are most likely to be frustrated. Unfortunately it has to be said that other organizations which have problems in common with parents of mentally-handicapped children are unlikely to welcome approaches from parents' groups fighting on behalf of their mentally-handicapped children. Despite sharing common problems other groups may fear (unreasonably of course) that they will be tainted by association with mental handicap. It is depressing to note that this represents a logical limit to the possibilities afforded to individual parents of mentally-handicapped children to cope with things by treating their child, and encouraging others to treat their child, as 'normally' as possible. And so parents of children who are physically disabled, blind or deaf who are also trying to bring up their child 'normally' will shy away from contact with mentally-handicapped children because this is not part of 'normality' (i.e. ordinary children do not regularly associate with mentally-handicapped children). Of course, it is what is generally accepted and not accepted as 'normality' that is a disgrace to humanity. And the more tenuous or indirect the common interest another self-help group has with mentally-handicapped children, the greater the possibility that it will deny it has anything in common with groups for the mentally-handicapped. But even within groups of people suffering the same disabling circumstances there can be hostility to the idea of associating with those who are most disabled. It has been known for sufferers from a particular progressive illness to have to set up two organizations because those with mild symptoms refused to associate with severe sufferers even though they themselves would eventually suffer severely! One suspects that similar attitudes could develop between parents of mentally-handicapped children, with parents of those children who can walk and talk not keen to be associated with 'special care' children with multiple handicaps. Neither is this to deny the depressing possibility that relatively affluent national voluntary bodies can also develop an inflexibility based on their own vested interests.

Despite the enormity of these problems, however, struggling to show other self-help groups what they have in common still seems to represent the best way forward. There seem to be several types of organization that parents of mentally-handicapped children could get to know and seek support from.

1.   Other local groups for the handicapped

These could include parent befriending groups; friends associations for both schools and training centres; groups for the mentally-handicapped (Mencap; Down's Association); groups for the physically-handicapped and able-bodied (PHAB); groups for the visually and hearing-impaired (the Royal National Institute for the Blind and for the Deaf).

These groups will have in common the experience of dealing with certain misinformed attitudes of the general public, though persuading each group that they share common problems may be a difficult task, as has been discussed.

2.   Other local groups for specific health difficulties
As well as the statutory Community Health Councils as part of each District Health Authority, these could include organizations supporting mental illness (MIND); progressive illness (Parkinson's Disease, multiple sclerosis); and epilepsy (British Epilepsy Association). Again, although there will be many differences, such groups may have many things in common. The mentally-ill have similar problems to the mentally-handicapped in the fight to obtain proper community care as an alternative to residential hospitals. Sufferers from Parkinson's Disease and cerebral palsy may have experiences to share over various drugs that they may have been given. Indeed how many mothers of a mentally-handicapped child are being prescribed a similar so-called 'minor tranquillizer' as their child? Whether, in each case, different groups can be encouraged to overcome their initial distaste for one another is another matter.

3.   Other local self-help organizations
One example of this could be a local Gingerbread group for one-parent families, who have in common with mothers of mentally-handicapped children decreased resources (in personnel if not also income), increased social isolation and a tendency to be labelled by professionals.

4.   Other groups for the handicapped in other areas
The importance of this is being able to compare services in different areas, so that parents who hear of a useful service in another area can ask for such a service in their own area.

5.   National groups for the mentally-handicapped
Groups such as Mencap and Campaign for People with

Mental Handicaps could provide groups with information and literature. Groups like Care and Home Farm Trust provide alternatives to adult-training centres and hospitals.

6.   National organizations for helping to deal with Services

A group like the National Association for the Welfare of Children in Hospital may be aimed at all children, but would have a great deal of relevance for mentally-handicapped children who have frequent stays in hospital. Various consumer groups might be enlisted to try to reduce the exorbitantly high profits that companies make from special equipment for the disabled.

7.   National organizations campaigning on relevant issues

These could include the Disability Alliance, fighting for a standard disability allowance, or the Child Poverty Action Group which argues on behalf of many forms of benefits affecting children. The National Council for Civil Liberties and the Children's Legal Centre have both campaigned for people's right of access to files written about them. Any initiative by trades unions to advocate paternity and maternity leave from work might be of interest to parents who have to take time off work on behalf of their handicapped child.

8.   Campaigning groups of professionals

Although much of this study has been involved in criticizing the viewpoint of some professionals, one has to consider all possibilities to create change. Parents can help by supporting those individuals who are going against most of the rest of their profession. For example, any educational psychologists, doctors and social workers who are beginning to argue for parents' access to files, could well do with parents' support.

I do not think that any of the proposals I have made in this study will be easy to implement. I am only too aware of the number of parents who point out how limited their time is, how the last thing they want to hear about are other people's problems when they have problems of their own, even how their children have different needs from other handicapped children. But the only alternative seems for parents to let professionals make decisions for them, which is what typically happens at present, with the issues largely out of parents' control.

List of Addresses of Organizations

MENCAP National Centre, 117 Golden Lane, London EC1.

Down's Children's Association, 4 Oxford Street, London W1.

Spastics Society, 12 Park Crescent, London W1N 4EQ.

PHAB, Tavistock House North, Tavistock Square, London WC1.

RNIB, 224 Great Portland Street, London W1N 6AA.

RNID, 105 Gower Street, London WC1E 6AH.

MIND, 22 Harley Street, London W1N 2ED.

Parkinson's Disease Society, 36 Portland Place, London W1.

Multiple Sclerosis Society, Fulham, London SW6.

British Epilepsy Association, New Wokingham Road, Berkshire, RG11 3AY.

Campaign for People with Mental Handicaps, 12a Maddox Street, London W1R 9PL.

CARE Central Office, 9A Weir Road, Kibworth, Leicestershire.

Home Farm Trust, General Manager, 57 Queens Square, Bristol, Avon.

National Association for the Welfare of Children in Hospital, Argyle House, Euston Road, London NW1.

An Open Letter to Parents

Disability Alliance, 25 Denmark Street, London WC2.

Child Poverty Action Group, 1-5 Bath Street, London
    EC1V 9QA.

National Council for Civil Liberties, 21 Tabard Street,
    London SE1 4LA.

Children's Legal Centre, 20 Compton Terrace, London N1.

Chapter Seven

AN OPEN LETTER TO PROFESSIONALS

(a) Introduction

In the analysis of the research, much has been said about the problems parents of the mentally-handicapped face in dealing with services and obtaining information. The analysis also included a few pointers as to how professional viewpoints and procedures seem to operate in this regard, sometimes seemingly making things more difficult for parents and child. Now, of course, there are a whole set of moral and political arguments one could put forward as a justification of why professionals should change the way they behave in certain respects. But perhaps of more importance to the professionals themselves are the practical reasons for changing which would help them in various ways. And always bearing in mind that modifying an absurd system is no substitute for wider political change, here are a few suggestions about the ways in which professionals might change their views and procedures. The emphasis on the medical profession is a reflection of the type of data looked at, which in turn owes something to the extent of medical involvement with mentally-handicapped children.

(b) Listening to the parents

"All health care workers should be encouraged to value the parental point of view." (Stacey, 1980, p. 87)

Now, doctors in particular may argue that they take

medical histories and therefore that they listen to parents in that way. But what they hear will be filtered through a very different training, perception and, often, social background from the parents. We have already seen how parents and doctors regard different issues as important. The question is not whether doctors listen to parents (they do, for their own purpose) but whether they will listen to issues the parents regard as relevant, and whether they can make the parents' worries central to their determinations.

GPs

(i)   Other research has suggested the need to educate General Practitioners to be aware of possible indications of handicap (Stacey, 1980, p. 87). This would seem even more necessary if such doctors are to continue to judge which families are entitled to the attendance allowance.

(ii) In any case a GP must feel able to refer parents who are worried to specialists. The GP might be reluctant to do this if he/she regards such worries as trivial, not wanting to waste either their own or a specialist's time. But it needs to be pointed out that not listening to parents' worries will waste more valuable medical time in the long run. It seems to me that the argument that a GP can train his/her clients not to ask for trivialities to be dealt with (Cartwright, 1967, p. 38), does not apply here in quite the same way. Firstly, the parents are worried on behalf of someone else (i.e. their child). And secondly, quite apart from their obvious concern as parents, there is the implicit threat that if they do not make certain of their child's 'best interests' at every step, there are increasing varieties of social agencies that can step in with the heavy hand of 'society-as-parent' (Fox, L., 1982, discusses this viewpoint). It seems likely, then, that if doctors do not listen to parents' worries at first, then they will simply have their time taken up again and again.

(iii) A GP may also be reluctant to refer parents and child to a specialist, if there are worries about how a specialist may respond to having his/her valuable time taken up. However, one paediatric clinic I observed demonstrated how it is possible to treat parents' worries seriously, even when the child proves to be quite ordinary. The paediatrician concerned spent 45 minutes with the parents and child, reassuring them about the child's stature by detailed physical examinations, reference to height and weight charts, comparisons with the parents' size, questions about diet and appetite etc. Afterwards the paediatrician told me that the mother must have been worried to persuade the GP to refer the child. He also pointed out that attending to the mother's worries now would save medical time eventually, as it would prevent problems later such as the mother feeding the child inappropriately. This seems to indicate that some doctors are already aware of the validity of the argument that listening to the parents, and taking their worries seriously is also in the best interests of the medical profession.

Paediatricians

(i) It has already been argued that encouraging doctors through their training to value the views of parents is not a guarantee that this will change the ways doctors practise As we have seen complaints that doctors do not listen to parents persist, despite parents quoting doctors as saying that they should listen more to parents, or even that their training taught them to listen to parents.

> M "When we do our training, he said, we are always told to listen to parents. They're the experts on their children." - Interview with parents.

(ii) Logically, if not practically, doctors might listen to parents if they had more time, which they could give themselves by agreeing with certain parents which recalls to paediatric clinics were achieving little and could be dispensed with.

(iii) But perhaps the best possibility for change lies in two different styles of clinic that seem to exist. One might be described as the comprehensive approach in which the doctor goes through a checklist of a whole series of examinations, questions, checks and tests. The other is more specific and aims to deal briefly with the concerns the doctor may have (e.g. the effect of drugs) and briefly with any concerns the parents ask about. Of course, all clinics in this study incorporated something of both these types in reality. Now some parents seem to find the comprehensive type reassuring at first, or when their child is young, but become disillusioned with the repetition of questions, often not linked to action, when the child is older. The more specific style saves time, but tends to rush by the parental point of view. In fact both styles crowd out the parental view to the extent that the doctor gets caught up in the routine of his/her particular style. One possibility would be to move from the comprehensive to the specific style as the child develops, but to use the comprehensive style in a modified way, to deal with specific worries of parents. The chances of parents being really listened to by paediatricians depend on the specific inclusion in the clinic routine of a space for asking parents what they think. The chances of including the parents' thoughts in the doctors' final deliberations depends on having established the precise relevance of a problem for parents by a comprehensive series of secondary questions (e.g. if a mother is worried about a child's low weight, then supplementary questions could be asked about diet, appetite, size and weight of parents, tendencies to diahorrea, allergies to types of food etc.) which simultaneously suggest or exclude certain solutions. And to the extent that the comprehensive style slows the pace of the clinic down, this might also increase the chances of parents being listened to.

(c) Taking Up Parents' Time

Paediatricians
    (i) The routine recall of parents and child to clinics which some parents find frustrating may be seen by paediatricians as good doctoring or as necessary because they feel accountable to medical colleagues, other professionals or hospital administrators.
    (ii) The rational solution of asking parents whether or not they feel their child is continuing to benefit from the clinics will seem less plausible to the doctors, so long as they believe that being a good professional means controlling decisions oneself.
    (iii) However, it would in theory be possible for paediatricians who wished to implement this policy to enlist the support of local parents' groups, local and national voluntary groups in persuading other doctors or administrators that asking parents about clinics was a

good idea.

(iv) At times of cuts in services paediatricians might be unwilling to initiate anything that would appear to reduce the numbers attending clinics and justify not replacing, say, the post of a junior doctor. It would perhaps be asking too much for doctors to argue to their health authorities that the better service they could give to others would be more efficient. Firstly, it would be efficient in the sense of being socially beneficial, rather than efficient in a narrow economic sense. Secondly, there is the whole question of whether it might be more beneficial to have more therapists or teachers rather than doctors in this instance. And thirdly, any argument the doctors might engage in on the efficiency of a service makes them unwilling actors in favour of a certain type of economic policy, and working towards helping parents and child then becomes even more difficult.

Assessment Centre

(i) Firstly, there is the question of whether the idea of assessment (residential or not) is one which parents find relevant in any way for their children. In this study the regular recall of children for a two-week residential assessment has many parallels to the routine paediatric clinics, particularly those in the comprehensive style. That is, parents seem to find them most useful the first or second time, and then usually when the child is very young. This would suggest a similar solution as that to the problem of routine recalls to the paediatric clinic, i.e. to use the comprehensive assessment when there is a specific problem in mind, and asking parents when they felt future assessment can be dispensed with. Indeed, one medical officer suggests something along these lines himself, as we have seen in chapter 4, pp. 95-6.

(ii) Secondly, there is the problem of the hospitalization of the child which various research has shown to be disturbing (and, by implication, counter-productive in the case of assessments) for both child and parents (Stacey et al, 1970). What the medical officer says about the duplication of services also suggests the solution to this problem. To the extent that psychologists, therapists, teachers, nurses, medical officers, and social workers already exist as community-based services, it seems possible that that proportion of work that these professionals give to children (usually living at home) who are temporarily resident in hospital for the assessment could become community-based, particularly if there was good co-operation with services already existing in the community. This would then avoid a situation where parents have to commit their child to a stressful residential period to obtain the services of these professionals. The possibility of moving those permanently (or near permanently) resident in the hospital to community hostels and home is a larger and much more complex issue (see also pp. 209-10).

(iii)   Thirdly, there is the issue of what is to be done if, for example, a health visitor or teacher feels that an assessment would be useful for the child but the parents do not. The only suggestion I can make here is that incidences of disagreement can be reduced by paying attention to the first two points (see also pp. 205-6).

(d)   Information

Paediatricians and other doctors
(i)   There seem to be good practical reasons, apart from any moral considerations, why doctors might make their own jobs easier in the long run by telling parents about any suspicions they have about a child's development. Delaying giving parents information because doctors are not quite sure and do not want to worry parents unnecessarily seems to me to be counter-productive from a medical point of view. This is because the doctors cannot then give parents genetic counselling or advice on contraception without alarming them anyway. And so parents may proceed to have further children in the meantime, as did two couples in this study, with the very real possibility that some of these children will be handicapped, and doctors will have compounded the problems they face. There is some suggestion that doctors should also tell parents about the suspicions they have over malformation as a cause of death in an infant, as research has indicated that such circumstances tended to hasten not deter the next pregnancy (Record and Armstrong, 1975, quoted in Philp and Duckworth, 1982, p. 93).

(ii)   Doctors might also make difficult situations easier for themselves by explaining the procedures they employ (e.g. regular clinics) to the parents, rather than being anxious about over-burdening them with information. This is because if the parents do not understand the reasons behind a doctor's actions, they will not be able to respond in the way that the doctor hopes. Firstly, they may misunderstand information they are given <u>because</u> the doctor has not been frank, and this may then make the doctor's task of persuasion all the more difficult, as this comment from a mother of a mentally-handicapped child illustrates:

> "I think (the doctors) probably tried to sound you out; I took him in when he was about three months and she was talking to him and holding him and his eyes were lighting up a little bit and she said, 'He is quite a bright boy for three months, isn't he?' Well now, instead of reacting as she hoped I would and saying 'Well now, I am rather worried', I clutched at that as a drowning man would at a straw and thought 'Thank God, there can't be anything wrong with him', and didn't say anything and just went home." (Hannam, 1980, p. 60)

And secondly, if parents are not told the reasons behind the procedures that the doctors use, they may think the procedures are irrelevant and cause more work for the doctors in the long run by failing to keep appointments, and so on.

(iii) The policy that some doctors adopt of waiting to see how a child develops in order not to worry the parents by expressing an opinion is also likely to have an effect opposite to the one intended. That is, a 'wait and see' policy will in itself worry the parents. Whether the parents have asked to see the doctor, or the doctor asked to see them the parents are <u>already</u> worried, and this may cause tensions because parents might reasonably interpret the situation as one of being ignored by the doctors. Again, the ill-feeling that may then be generated need not happen if procedures are explained to parents, and the doctors' task will become that much easier.

(iv) It has already been argued that by not telling parents of their own uncertainties, doctors will put pressure on themselves by encouraging parents to expect the impossible, that is for a doctor to have 100%

knowledge about a situation. Similarly, labelling a child in a once-and-for-all manner puts unnecessary pressure on doctors, as well as alienating the parents if events turn out otherwise.

(v) Now, one doctor in the study argued that sometimes labelling a child was a form of reverse psychology in which a doctor tries to get the parents to react determinedly against the pronouncement and thus stimulate the child to the greatest possible extent. Quite apart from the dubious morality of such a venture, we have just seen (p. 200) that attempting to manipulate the reactions of parents can have the opposite effect from the one intended.

The Files of Professionals in General

(i)   There are many practical reasons why professionals of all kinds could improve both the service they give and the quality of their working conditions by allowing clients access to files written about them (i.e. open files). Now, there are two reasons why in the case of mentally-handicapped children the principle of open files should mean that the parents are allowed to read them. Firstly, as far as we know at the moment, the children are unlikely to be able to read the files themselves, and the parents (or foster parents) would be many people's first choice as the child's representatives. And secondly, in this study, the files contain at least as much comment about the parents as about the child, and to that extent the parents are as much the clients as the child.

(ii)   On the basis that some parents say that they worry about not knowing what is written in professional reports, and trust those professionals who are open about giving them information, opening up the files would arguably cut down the demands made on professionals' time by parents who are unsure what is going on.

(iii)   If, by being able to read in the files what professionals really think of them and their child, parents come to place even greater trust in the professionals, this would mean that the professionals' files would be more complete and accurate. The files would be more complete because, knowing they could check the validity of what was written, parents would be more likely to tell professionals things. And the files would be more accurate because any misunderstandings or inaccuracies could be pointed out by the parents. If the professionals are worried that only the more articulate and middle-class parents would ask to see their files, thereby putting less assertive parents at a disadvantage, copies of letters could be sent to parents in the same way that copies are presently sent to five or six other professionals or authorities.

(iv) Allowing the parents to read the files would also help protect the professional from unwarranted accusations of negligence. Giving the parents a greater sense of responsibility might also give them a greater sense of control over their own and their child's affairs, such that they would be less inclined to blame anyone if things went wrong, than if professionals had taken on all the responsibility themselves.

(v) It is interesting to note that one of the first consequences of open files in practice is that the professionals are more careful and considerate in what they write, as illustrated in Chapter 6, p. 181.

(vi) Indeed this increased sensitivity seems to lead the professionals to consider the impact of what they are writing, as also mentioned in Chapter 6, p. 181.

(vii) Given that part of professional training emphasizes how professionals should keep their emotions in check, but also that in the area of mental handicap some of the work that all professionals do will be distressing, there is a danger that closed and secret files will be an outlet for certain emotions of the professionals, perhaps without them fully realizing this. For example, if professionals are upset when parents reject a handicapped child because they know only too well the limitations of growing up on a hospital ward and feel sorry for the child, then changing the way they write about the parents (one consultant claimed he was less discursive in such instances) is not a productive way of channelling emotions. If emotions are hidden away in different styles of records, then there can be no initiatives taken to help professionals cope with what are very emotionally draining occupations by establishing group discussions, support networks or even group therapy for the professionals involved.

(viii) Doctors may worry about parents becoming aware of disagreements between professionals as to clinical judgements. But if this is so, doctors are then less likely to label a child so quickly in a once-and-for-all manner, perhaps suggesting a professional opinion instead.

This would not only recognize that doctors are not always clinically correct in a way less harmful to the profession than the more sensational manner when dogmatic assertions prove to be incorrect. It would also demonstrate how often the professional medical opinion is well-considered. At a time when relations between professionals and clients are coming under increasing scrutiny, this would help demonstrate the continued worth of professionals to enjoy a high regard (but not reward) in society.

(ix)   Open files would also enable certain conceptual confusions in professionals' thinking to be removed. For example, many different professionals, including doctors, use the term 'Educational Sub-Normality' as if it were an eternal truth, instead of what it is - a legal/educational term, developed at a certain specific point in history, and open to such wildly variable interpretation as to make it utterly meaningless (see Chapter 6, p. 182).

The Case-Conferences of Professionals in General

(i)   In a way the distinction drawn here between files and case-conferences is an arbitrary one. Most of the arguments put forward about access to professional files also apply with regard to access to case-conferences and vice-versa.

(ii)   If parents are allowed into all case-conferences held about their child, and also for the entire duration of each case-conference then one of the advantages for the professionals will be that they will have to use clear and non-technical language so that the parents can understand. Now of course the ability to express oneself clearly in ordinary language, avoiding technical jargon, is in itself one measure of professional competence, (a measure which would surely indict Chapter 6). But using ordinary language in case-conferences will help professionals to give a better service in other ways. It seems likely that using uncomplicated language will encourage more practical suggestions, given what the parents say about the simple, straightforward suggestions being the most useful (see p. 32). Also, plain language will be more likely to encourage practical ideas and suggestions from other professionals, who will not have to deal with professional jargon as an obstacle to clear communication.

(iii)   Having the parents present at case-conferences will also help the professionals by saving them time. Any half-formed ideas that professionals put forward for discussion may be quickly shown up by the parents if the ideas are unsuitable, or miss the point, or fail to take something into account that is very obvious to the parents. There is the possibility of parents not acknowledging what problems there are in some circumstances. But then all the more reason to have the parents present. Take a hypothetical extreme example, where the professionals suspect the child has suffered non-accidental injury. The earlier the parents are confronted with this, the earlier the child is saved from further hardship, and the earlier the relevant professionals can get to the root of the problem and offer help. This brings us to the possibility that parents will be angry with professionals for making certain suggestions, and of course professionals deserve the full protection of the law. But many people's occupation leaves them open to some anger from the public, and it seems a small price to pay to ensure the well-being of a child. In such extreme instances the secrecy that would be involved in excluding parents from case-conferences reverse the democratic principle of being presumed innocent until proven guilty.

(iv) By including parents in case-conferences, professionals could also provide a useful service in helping parents not to worry, however contrary to popular belief this may seem. Any worries that parents have will exist already, simply by virtue of the case-conference being held. Being excluded from all, or part of any case-conference will increase their anxiety because they feel they do not know what is really being said. Parents in this study claim that in general they do not have time to worry because they are too involved in the practical day-to-day care of their child. On this basis it seems plausible to argue that by involving parents fully in any case-conference on their child, rather than have them wait in a room next door, for example, the professionals could perform a great service by reducing their anxieties.

(v) Any fears that parents could be intimidated by the close questioning from professionals could be resolved by allowing parents to be accompanied by a friend, representative or adviser. If (as one doctor in this study suggested) some professionals really cannot be trusted not to ask unwarranted personal and revealing questions of the parents, then including a representative would seem preferable from the professional point of view, as the alternative might be a consideration of whether case-conferences are appropriate institutions at all.

(vi)   Of course, professionals who propose to include parents in all case-conferences may face accusations of being politically motivated, from other professionals who are equally politically motivated, either in excluding parents, or in trying to define the issue as outside politics. Let us extend a point made by Pheby in relation to medical records.

> "... The present secrecy, in the absence of any other checks or balances, may have encouraged an irresponsible attitude to develop on the part of some practitioners, and (...) it is up to the medical profession, if it wishes to maintain the present position with regard to medical records, to devise suitable safeguards for the interests of patients." (Pheby, 1982, p. 17)

It is up to professionals to ensure that the interests of clients are safeguarded by recognizing that any procedures enshrined in case-conferences have wider political implications (see p. 204) on the question of being innocent until proven guilty), if those professionals wish to continue to have a persuasive voice in the way they distribute their services.

(e)   Assessing a Child

Assessment Centre/Paediatricians/Medical Officers/
Educational Psychologists
    (i)   Various estimations of a child's ability by strangers in unfamiliar settings are generally disliked by the parents. Professionals seem to argue that parents typically complain about the inappropriate circumstances of the tests, and that anyway the conditions are the same for all children. But we have seen that these are not fair arguments since the ordinary child is left out of account (see Chapter 4, pp. 92-4). In any case, it is in the interests of the professionals to take notice of the criticisms parents make of the circumstance for testing. After all, professionals want the parents to follow their recommendations, and this depends on convincing the parents on their own terms. This in turn means profes-

sionals and parents must agree on which criteria are important.

(ii)   Since many of the parents' concerns are to do with practical difficulties, agreeing with parents which criteria are important in testing may enable test items to be better linked to practical solutions.

(f)   Insensitive Attitudes

Paediatricians and other hospital specialists

(i)   Although most specialists have been separated from the experience of mentally-handicapped children (through privileged training; relative isolation from the community through being based in hospital; rarely dealing with such children as patients etc.) this applies somewhat less to paediatricians who obviously have more contact with the mentally-handicapped. This helps to explain why most (but by no means all) of the criticism for being insensitive is directed at hospital specialists other than paediatricians. This would seem to suggest one possible strategy, whereby paediatricians were responsible for educating their less sensitive colleagues through some form of in-service training.

(ii)   Given the experience of some mothers of realizing something was wrong because they were treated sensitively at a time when they expected to be treated routinely, this suggests that putting aside usual medical routine, making a special fuss, making a point of being sensitive are possible ways of beginning the difficult task of breaking bad news to the parents.

(g)   Routines

Paediatric Clinics

(i)   It has already been argued that allowing parents to withdraw from routine recall clinics would save paediatricians' time and lead to a decrease in the number who fail to keep appointments.

(ii)   The problem of parents' dissatisfaction when seen by the paediatrician's assistants or junior doctors is a difficult one, as paediatricians in this study recognize, making as they do an effort for the parents to be seen by themselves as well as, or instead of, their assistants if specially requested. But as long as the careers of doctors depend on training through the various hierarchies of medicine any solutions will only be partial. At present doctors are perpetuating a system where their own time is wasted. If parents are seen by an assistant and are dissatisfied they may ask to be seen again anyway, or they may feel attending is a waste of their time, and so not keep appointments, and waste the doctors' time in that way.

Medical Officers and Educational Psychologists

(i)   As two types of professionals whose roles and procedures the parents in this study generally feel they do not understand, both have an interest in explaining their routines so that parents do not misunderstand the information they are given or view the routines as irrelevant (see pp. 199-200).

(ii)   Both medical officers and educational psychologists could make their obligations with regard to decisions about schooling less of a problem by informing the parents that they are to be involved with the child, that they have begun to keep records on the child, and that they will keep the parents fully informed about when, how and for what purpose they propose to continue to see the child at school. This would avoid the hostility and resentment which is caused when parents find out that professionals have seen their child without their prior knowledge. Parents are less likely to have a favourable view of a special school if certain professionals treat children who attend such schools as 'fair game' for their tests, assessments or profiles without seeking the permission of the parents. At the moment the professionals are only making their responsibilities for deciding on schooling more difficult for themselves to implement.

(h) Lack of Services

Therapists (Speech, Occupational and Physio)

(i)   Given that these various forms of therapy were generally agreed to be useful by parents in this study, the practice of having clients referred to them by other professionals, such as doctors, does seem a drawback. But since this is the case, those who can refer people to therapists need to be educated about the entire range of ways in which therapists can be useful for mentally-handicapped children.

The ways in which some doctors view physiotherapy as trivial has been discussed above (Chapter 4, pp. 122-3). But physiotherapy is valuable to mentally-handicapped children in many ways not apparently recognized by some doctors. Spastic limbs can be exercised in specific ways to prevent deterioration and the consequent increased difficulty of handling the child. Mistakes such as encouraging a child to walk, when the effort is causing the grating together of bones in the ankle, can be avoided. Cerebral palsied children who cannot talk can only demonstrate their intelligence clearly by, say, pointing, which depends on the increased control of an arm which physiotherapy could help develop. Even such a simple matter as finding the most comfortable position for a child who cannot walk depends on knowledge which physiotherapists have at their disposal.

(ii)   Meanwhile, let us consider some general reasons why parents in this study find therapy services useful. It seems to be because they offer simple, practically-oriented advice and service, that can involve the parents, and is well-suited to being given as a community service. However, it is possible that in search of better pay and status therapy professionals will attempt to become more like some doctors and psychologists: more technical; emphasizing status within the profession depending on what type of client one deals with (dealing with mentally-handicapped people would be low status); perhaps hospital-based. All of which would tend to make them less useful to the parents and child. The only way to prevent this would be for health, education and social services authorities to recognize the value of the type of work they do now in term of pay and prestige.

Teachers

A similar type of argument applies to the teachers at ESN(S) schools. The services they provide which parents find most useful are the informal, supportive roles (e.g. taking the children on holiday, looking after parents' other children when parents are up at the school, sometimes even child-minding after school or at weekends). At present, the financially hard-pressed social services are prepared to unofficially depend on the good nature of these (women) teachers. However, with moves apparent to become more 'professional' (both to offer a better educational service and to claim greater pay and prestige) such informal support will become less possible. It is, therefore, important that as the teachers attempt to achieve greater professional status that formal statutory services are developed to replace their informal work, or that this work is recognized as valuable and paid for.

(i) Appropriateness of Services

'Phased-Care' in Hospital

Some parents found this system useful, others used it reluctantly, and some would not make use of this form of relief because it was hospital-based. The doctors at the hospital where phased-care was offered claimed that one major benefit was to decrease the numbers who were to be looked after in hospital on a permanent or near-permanent basis. But these very terms suggest that the best way to achieve this lies in the provision of relief care in various forms in the community (see pp. 87-8). The take-up of relief care would then be that much greater which would decrease the need for permanent or near-permanent care in several related ways. Firstly, fewer families would submit themselves to the stress of coping permanently at home, which might conceivably lead to a fall in the numbers of break-ups, mental or physical illnesses, or other family crises which might lead not only to permanent care in hospital, but a particularly traumatic admission for a child/adult used only to care at home. Secondly, it is possible that by being more visible to the general public through living in the community than in residential hospitals the stigma surrounding mentally-handicapped people could be lessened. And thirdly reducing the relative social isolation of the parents might also reduce such stigma by reducing the overall associated stigma accorded to families of the mentally-handicapped. (Goffman, 1968, p. 31 refers to the 'courtesy stigma' that friends and relatives of the handicapped are given by others.) Of course, the community care envisaged must be distinguished from the sham notion of care in the community where the burden of work is returned predominantly to the mother on the spurious assumption that friends, neighbours and relatives will provide support (shown to be a myth by Wilkin, 1979). But equally the genuine concern of hospital staff that their role will be reduced without the necessary resources going into the community can become a justification for keeping things the way they are.

Social Workers

To judge by the positive response of those parents who had had the opportunity to attend one of the series of group meetings run by two social workers, the main help such workers can offer is to give information about benefits and services and to put young parents in contact with one another, especially at an early stage in the child's life. Beyond such help, however, social workers come up against problems of a similar nature to those discussed in other research, namely a tendency to look for psychological insights to problems that they either cannot alter because of the conditions of the wider society, or which are really financial and economic problems (Mayer and Timms, 1970, p. 141). This is the stage where social workers appear to the parents to be in effect adding the extra stigma of social work involvement to the problems of trying to bring up a mentally-handicapped child. But given the potential of social workers to offer families help in the early stages, doctors must find a solution to their dilemma of not referring families to social workers because of confidentiality. The best way of doing this seems to be to let the parents know that special group meetings can be arranged where they can receive information about services and benefits and meet other parents, and thereby encourage parents to refer themselves to the social workers. The present arrangement in this study of an indirect link from social workers to medical officer to health visitors to parents seems unsatisfactory. There is some suggestion from parents themselves that professional jealousies meant that health visitors informed the parents, but also discouraged them from agreeing to such meetings. This seems to me to indicate a more general problem: where professionals of all kinds are worried they are not doing enough for the parents, they may want to be the ones who give the most precious information, e.g. the attendance allowance. Therefore, a system where doctors, especially after paediatric clinics, gave parents an explanatory leaflet inviting them to refer themselves to social workers for such meetings might be referable. Stacey (1980) has suggested that "literature should be on display near the area where people sit" (p. 83).

(j) Alternatives

All professionals

The issues here seems to be <u>not</u> to suggest to various professionals what alternatives they can offer parents within the given constraints of the bureaucratic and legal procedures they administer, but to demonstrate to those professionals the ways in which those procedures effectively give parents no realistic choice, perhaps contrary to what the professionals themselves believe. For example, the parents are effectively given no choice about schooling.

To illustrate this, let us consider the Conservative Government's record on the handicapped, in which a brief acknowledgement of the integration viewpoint in the 1980 White Paper becomes a vigorous reinforcement of the principle of segregation in the 1981 Education Act because the aims of the British educational system are neither stated nor questioned. Section 35 of the White Paper begins:

> "There are legitimate differences of view over where and how a child with special educational needs is best educated. The Government takes as its starting point the principle that children and young people who have such needs should be educated in association with those who do not."

However, section 35 goes on to argue that:

> " ... this principle must always be applied so as not to frustrate the aim of giving the child or student, within the limits of what is practicable, the greatest possible opportunity to benefit from the education process."

This suggests that integration should depend on the <u>child</u> being <u>free in practice</u> to derive the maximum

211

benefit from the educational system. Yet one of the reasons that the Government decided not to implement the pro-integration section 10 of the 1976 Education Act is that:

> "It gives no opportunity to the expression of parental preference." (section 36)

So integration is being rejected on the ground that the <u>parents</u> must be <u>free in practice</u>. Similarly section 35 of the White Paper suggests that the <u>professionals</u> and <u>parents</u> should be involved in <u>democratic decision-making</u> over the educational placement of a child judged to have special needs:

> "The right placement for a child with a serious disability can only be properly determined after careful assessment of his needs by competent professionals and in close consultation with his parents."

Yet in the next sentence comprehensive integration (or association as it is referred to) is rejected on grounds which suggest it would be <u>undemocratic decision-making</u> which did not refer to <u>other children</u> and <u>the taxpayer:</u>

> "For some children with special needs association, or full association, with other children is the wrong solution and to impose it would be unfair to the child, his parents, other children and the taxpayer."

As we have already seen, section 35 of the 1980 White Paper seems to argue that children with special educational needs should be <u>equal</u> to those without in <u>principle</u>:

> "The Government takes as its starting point the principle that children and young people who have such needs should be educated in association with those who do not."

But the terms of the 1981 Education Act ensure that equality in principle can never mean integration and equality in practice because of section 2(3) of the Act which states the conditions under which a child with special educational needs may be educated in an ordinary school. Educating the child in an ordinary school must be compatible with:

> "(a) his receiving the special educational provision that he requires."

Therefore, local education authorities are granted an immense power simply to argue that special educational provision can only be provided in segregated special schools. This is because there is no requirement made on local education authorities to make special educational provision in ordinary schools. This constitutes a very crucial difference from what the Act actually says which is that where possible children with special educational needs should be educated in ordinary schools. This lack of requirement could arguably be said to be a devious evasion of the crucial issues. Secondly, such special provision should also be compatible with:

> "(b) the provision of efficient education for the children with whom he will be educated."

Again, equality in principle becomes inequality in practice and at the same time reveals what is being taken for granted in the debate, that is the aims of the ordinary schooling system. The educational system in Britain is characterized by various forms of segregation. In addition to the separate public schools creating a self-defining elite, there are schools for slow learners, the maladjusted, the physically disabled and the mentally-handicapped. But such segregation did not come about through goodwill for any of these latter groups, and there are good historical reasons for taking what may appear at first to be a cynical attitude. Firstly, to deal with the origins of special provision for those we now refer to as 'mentally-handicapped' or 'ESN(S)' children.

> "The tendency, beginning in the seventeenth century, to confine paupers and the unemployed to the workhouse, had drawn in numbers of defective children who interrupted the smooth functioning of forced labour and set problems for

> the workhouse guardians (...) the setting up of separate institutions for the mentally-defective, to give some kind of instruction and trade training, served a variety of interests. Economic interests were served by removing defective people who were interrupting the workhouse labour, but also the possibility of training mentally-defective people for productive work was important. Political interests were served by the removal into residential care and confinement of a potentially disruptive social group."
> (Tomlinson, 1982, p. 39)

And secondly, to deal with those we now call 'slow learners' or ESN(M) children:

> "It was the introduction of state compulsory education in the 1870s that focussed attention more acutely on children who were not idiots or imbeciles, but who experienced difficulty with a formal educational system. Again, state intervention in discovering these dull and troublesome children was not necessarily for their own 'good' or a recognition of their 'needs'. It was primarily to ensure the smoother running of the normal educational system." (Tomlinson, 1982, p. 42)

These concerns have remained as a legacy to the segregated educational system that we have in Britain today. But there is a further twist to the way this segregation works. Some of the children separated from one another by virtue of the existence of special schools come together as adults (or with the next generation of special school children) - some as professionals and others as their clients. Pupils in ordinary schools who are to become doctors, psychiatrists, teachers, psychologists or researchers begin their education in classes excluding their future clients: the physically disabled, the mentally-handicapped, slow learners etc. The educational system is thus another factor in the development of people into professionals and those who will be permanently dependent as clients. Furthermore, the professionals are expected to learn ways of thinking about a group of clients when they have been systematically excluded from one another's experiences. Not surprisingly the professionals tend to see the problems of the client group in terms of their deficiencies relative to the professionals' own experiences. In short, the knowledge that professionals gain through school and university depends on special schools, segregated from the rest of the educational system. By this I mean that learning very abstract types of knowledge depends on excluding from classes those who seemingly cannot learn such knowledge and who it is feared would disrupt teaching as it is constituted by the current educational system. Talk of 'efficient education' in the 1981 Act ignores this relationship, and appeals to commonsense assumptions that a severely mentally-handicapped child cannot possibly be taught alongside an ordinary child (for whom the lesson is a necessary step towards the possibility of later being trained as a professional). I say 'commonsense assumptions' because there is a question here that is being both asked and answered and then hidden from view so that it can never be critically examined. The question is: segregation through special schools or hold back the intellectual development of ordinary schoolchildren? The question suggests that future professionals have an interest in the handicapped being separated (i.e. they have opposing interests). But how are we to reconcile these opposing interests with the claim that later there will be agreement and harmony in the professional-client relationship? Why does an opposition of interests as children become a common interest for the adult professional and the next generation of mentally-handicapped children? The short answer is that it cannot, and that the question of segregation versus holding back intelligence is a misconception. It is a misconception because it assumes that the best way to train a professional is through abstract theory (school and university) and at a very late stage observation (watching other professionals) and trial and error (practising being a professional). One alternative is to learn through the social experience of continually finding ways of being with and relating to a mentally-handicapped person as one grows up.

The true problem is a broad social one of how people organize their lives, not an unfortunate gap in professional knowledge. For doctors this gap is supposed to be between medicine being able to save severely mentally-handicapped babies at birth, when previously many would have died, and a time in the future when genetic counselling, screening, abortion or in vitro fertilization ('test-tube baby' techniques) will mean hardly any babies will be born who have a severe mental disability. Indeed, in vitro fertilization is as much a cause for concern as rejoicing. In years to come it may be that techniques will be developed to decrease the number of babies born with mental or physical defects. But there is some evidence that professionals act most sensitively and kindly when they either do not know or cannot control what is wrong. Such is the case with professionals and mentally-handicapped children today. But this suggests that in the future the fewer handicapped who are born will be in danger of being treated very badly by society when there is greater control and knowledge of what is wrong. This seems to me to be a good reason to analyse the problems from a social point of view.

Finally, the 1981 Education Act says that educating the child in an ordinary school must be compatible with:

> "(c)   the efficient use of resources."

This derives from our society's valuing only the economically useful and productive individual. It also appeals to the idea that 'the taxpayer' equals everyone and is, therefore, the common interest. But the mentally-handicapped, and their mothers who perform most of the work in caring for them, do not usually pay tax because they are not paid in the first place for the work that they do.

As long as the aims of those who control the educational system in Britain remain hidden and not open to discussion, people come to regard segregated schooling as something 'natural', i.e. the existence of special schools is completely unquestioned. Now, a state of affairs that is seen as 'natural' is also seen as above or beyond politics. But a question that deals with an issue such as how we are to live our lives, involving and affecting us all (which is, after all, what the aim of the education system in Britain is) is by definition political. The word 'political' is derived from the Greek word 'politikos' meaning popular; of the people; carried on by the people. So what is in fact a political question has come to be defined as outside politics, and since this defining out is based on institutional arrangements in the real world (i.e. segregated schooling) anyone who then tries to argue that it is a political question can be portrayed as an evil political hack who wants to force a political point at the expense of 'the best interests of a child with special needs'. Such people can, and indeed have been, portrayed as:

(i) Anti-democracy - accused of trying to destroy the consensus between professionals and parents, when in actual fact decisions about educational placement generally are made in the 'interests' (as they are currently socially defined) of the taxpayer and the ordinary schoolchild. What is being challenged, however, is not the consensus but the illusion of the consensus.

(ii) Anti-equality - accused of not being fair to the handicapped child, of not taking account of its special interests. But it is in the interests of the ordinary schoolchild to distinguish between the interests of the ordinary schoolchild and the mentally-handicapped schoolchild in the first place.

(iii) Anti-freedom - accused of imposing one's own will on the parents. As soon as parents of handicapped children find a voice and begin to make suggestions about the services for their children, the professionals do not believe that the parents are motivated to have done this on their own, and assume that they are being politically manipulated by an intellectual/political extremist/ trouble-maker. Which is patronizing to the extent of implying that the parents are not capable of thinking for themselves.

(k) Conclusion

Although many criticisms of professionalized services have been put forward here, this does not necessarily imply criticisms of individual personnel. After all, Johnson (1972, p. 38) argues that the professional form of occupational control was historically specific to the 'laissez-faire' period of the nineteenth century, and that now many services are mediated through the state and state bureaucracies. No doubt many professionals feel the kind of frustrations over bureaucratic requirements that Cartwright (1967, p. 59) reports for GPs. It must then seem very harsh to be criticized when professionals feel they are tied by bureaucratic, administrative, inter-professional and political necessities, and cannot function quite as they wish. But having said this, doctors and psychologists (and to a lesser extent social workers and teachers) enjoy state training and education, high status, considerable material reward and relatively greater levels of control over their working conditions than many other occupations. Though they may feel constrained in many ways, they are in a far stronger position to influence situations than are either the parents or their mentally-handicapped children. If professionals really feel frustrated by bureaucratic restrictions, then arguably one reasonable argument they can draw upon is to show how this affects parents and children in terms of what the parents themselves say. It is certainly true that on occasions the interests of the parents may be different from those of the child. But consider the frustrations that professionals feel when subject to restrictions from administrators or other professionals (who, it may be felt, are not in a position to understand the practicalities of a particular form of professional work). Multiply these frustrations several times over, and you can only begin to appreciate the torment of a mother who, involved in the constant care of her mentally-handicapped child, finds that her viewpoint is not even taken seriously, let alone made central to the distribution of services.

Appendices

The Sample
The twenty children around whom the study was based
were the most recent twenty recorded on the register of
one ESN(S) school where the total number of children
attending the school was approximately forty-five. This
strategy excluded three two-year-olds who were attending
the school informally on a part-time basis (the extent of
their disability was not certain) and who were therefore
not on the register. However, this also meant including
three children originally born outside the school catchment
area which the parents had subsequently moved to. In one
case this was from a neighbouring county and in two cases
from abroad. The sample also included an older child who
had only recently started attending regularly and been put
on the school register.

Files
Access to the files on the twenty children was arranged
through the following professionals respectively:

ESN(S) School .... Head-teacher
Community Health Services .... Senior Clinical
Medical Officer
General Hospital .... 3 Consultant
Paediatricians
Assessment Hospital .... Consultant
Schools Psychological Service .... Senior Educational
Psychologist

The files were researched by taking extracts from the
letters contained there, letters written from one
professional to another. Copies of letters had often been
sent to all the relevant professionals, so that sometimes I
had seen the same letter in several different files by the
time I had reviewed all the files. The more technical
contents of the files (e.g. test schedules, X-rays,
pathology lab. cards, hospital ward admission cards etc.)
were noted down as existing without trying to take details
from them.
With regard to the school, the psychological service
and the community health services, the files of all twenty

children were looked at. Seventeen general hospital files were reviewed - one child had never been seen regularly by a paediatrician, one had not been seen by the local paediatricians and one was excluded at the request of a paediatrician. Only fourteen of the children had been involved with the assessment hospital, of whom only twelve of the parents gave written permission for me to see the files. Two of these had no notes, and one was omitted at the request of the consultant which left nine to be reviewed. Social services refused me permission to look at any files, and as most parents had not been in contact with a social worker, and of those who had it was for reasons other then having a mentally-handicapped child (e.g. being foster-parents) it was decided not to pursue the matter.

The Clinics

Twelve children were seen in the paediatricians' clinics. Four no longer attended paediatric clinics, in one case the parents did not wish me to tape the clinic, and one was excluded at the request of the paediatrician. The remaining two were missed by not contacting the parents early enough to establish when the clinics were.

The Meetings

These depended largely on what was made available to me by the professionals. The clincial medical officer, for example, no longer saw all the children regularly and as far as I could tell simply selected the first two children he was due to see after he had agreed to me accompanying him. Similarly, the educational psychologist did not meet the parents on any systematized or regular basis and the two meetings I taped were again the first two that occurred after we had agreed permission in principle. And again, the educational case-conferences (reviews) taped were the first four to take place after I had obtained permission in principle.

Appendices

APPENDIX 2

Research completed in respect of each individual family *

	Interview	Files					Clinics	Educational Reviews	Meeting with Psychologist	Assessment by Medical Officer	Apology and Permission	Report	TOTAL no. of contacts
		School	Psychology Service	Community Health	General Hospital	Assessment Hospital							
1	*	*	*	*							*	*	6
2	*	*	*	*	*		*		*		*	*	9
3	*	*	*	*	*	*	*				*	*	9
4	*	*	*	*	*	*	*	*			*	*	10
5	*	*	*	*	*	*					*	*	8
6	*	*	*	*	*	*	*	*			*	*	10
7	*	*	*	*	*	*	*				*	*	9
8	*	*	*	*	*	*	*	*			*	*	10
9	*	*	*	*	*						*	*	7
10	*	*	*	*	*	*					*	*	8
11	*	*	*	*	*	*	*				*	*	9
12	*	*	*	*	*	*	*				*	*	9
13	*	*	*	*				*			*	*	7
14	*	*	*	*							*	*	6
15	*	*	*	*	*						*	*	7
16	*	*	*	*	*		*		*		*	*	9
17	*	*	*	*	*		*			*	*	*	9
18	*	*	*	*	*					*	*	*	8
19	*	*	*	*	*		*				*	*	8
20	*	*	*	*	*		*				*	*	8
Total	20	20	20	20	17	9	12	4	2	2	20	20	

APPENDIX 3

Letter to the Parents Requesting an Interview
The letter was typed on University of Warwick notepaper and also included an address and telephone number for the area where the research took place. The text of the letter was as follows.

Dear (Name of Parents)

I am writing to you as a postgraduate student in the Department of Sociology, University of Warwick. My research project is aimed at the study of various professional services available to families of children attending special schools. I understand that (name of child) is at present attending (name of ESN(S) school). I feel that it is very important to understand the point of view and opinions of the parents and I wonder if it would therefore be possible for me to record a taped interview with you at your home? The information gained would be treated in the strictest confidence and your name would not be divulged in any academic papers subsequently written. I shall, of course, confirm permission for this approach with (name of head-teacher). Below is a date and time at which I would like to call if this is convenient with you. Please feel free to return the stamped addressed envelope if you would like to arrange an alternative day and time. Meanwhile, you are welcome to contact the above number if you wish to confirm my identity.

I look forward to meeting you on (proposed date) at (proposed time). Thank you for your co-operation,

Yours sincerely

SIMON DYSON

APPENDIX 4

Checklist used for Taped Interviews

WHEN DID YOU FIRST SUSPECT SOMETHING WAS THE MATTER?

Why suspect? What do? How feel?

WHAT PRACTICAL PROBLEMS DID YOU HAVE?

At first? Later? Now?

WHAT WAS THE FIRST SERVICE YOU WERE IN CONTACT WITH?

When contacted? What advice/help given?

HAVE YOU HAD ANY CONTACT WITH OTHER SERVICES?

Family Doctor
Paediatrician
Pre-School Services
Medical Officer
Special School
Educational Psychologist
Social Services
Assessment Unit / Residential Hospital
Other Services (Therapists)

When contacted? What advice/help given?

HAVE YOU HAD ANY CONTACT WITH VOLUNTARY SERVICES?

Mencap? Rowntree Trust? Others?

DID YOU HAVE ANY PRACTICAL PROBLEMS IN RELATION TO THE SERVICES?

Transport? Time off work? Waiting?

ANY SERVICES NOT AVAILABLE THAT WOULD BE USEFUL?

EXPECTATIONS OF THE FUTURE?

Hopes? Concerns? Knowledge of services available?

WHAT ALLOWANCES DO YOU RECEIVE?

Attendance allowance? Mobility Allowance? How told about them?

WHAT OTHER CONTACTS DO YOU HAVE?

Teachers? Other Parents?

ANY OTHER COMMENTS?

About services? About this interview?

APPENDIX 5

Socio-economic Status of Families by Father's Occupation

Registrar General's Classification	Number of Families
I	1
II	3
III Non-Manual	0
III Manual	6
IV	4
V	3
Unknown	3
Total	20

Source: School Files

BIBLIOGRAPHY

Acts of Parliament

Education Act (1976), London: HMSO
Education Act (1981), London: HMSO

Barton, L. and Tomlinson, S. (eds) (1981), Special Education: Policy, Practices and Social Issues, London: Harper and Row

Booth, Tony and Statham, J. (1982), The Nature of Special Education, London: Croom Helm/Open University Press

Booth, Tony and Swann, W. (eds) (1987) Including Pupils with Disabilities, Open University Press

British Medical Association and Pharmaceutical Society of Great Britain (1981), British National Formulary, No. 2

Cartwright, A. (1967), Patients and their Doctors: A Study of General Practice, London: Routledge and Kegan Paul

Cartwright, A. and Anderson, R. (1981), General Practice Revisited - A Second Study of Patients and their Doctors, London: Tavistock

Cohen, R. (1982), Whose File is it Anyway?, London: National Council for Civil Liberties

Davis, A. G. (1982), Children in Clinics: A Sociological Analysis of Medical Work with Children, London: Tavistock

Davis, F. (1963), Passage Through Crisis: Polio victims and their families, New York: Bobbs-Merrill

Dyson, S. M. (1986), "Professionals, Mentally-Handicapped Children and Confidential Files", Disability, Handicap and Society 1 (1) 73-87

Dyson, S. M. (1987), "Reasons for Assessment: Rhetoric and Reality in the Assessment of Children with Disabilities" in Booth, Tony and Swann, W. (eds) (1987) Chapter 16

Dyson, S. M. (1981), "The Theory and Practice of Intelligence Testing and the Career of the ESN(M) Child", unpublished dissertation, Department of Sociology, University of Leicester

226

Family Focus (1982) Parental Involvement with the Assessment of Children with Special Needs, Coventry, May 1982

Fox, L. M. (1982), "Two Value Positions in Recent Child Care Law and Practice", British Journal of Social Work 12 265-90

Goffman, E. (1968), Stigma: the management of spoilt identity, Harmondsworth: Penguin

Hannam, C. (1980), Parents and Mentally-handicapped Children, Harmondsworth: Penguin (second edition)

Johnson, T. (1972), Professions and Power, London: Macmillan

Mayer, J. and Timms, N. (1970), The Client Speaks: Working-Class Impressions of Casework, London: Routledge and Kegan Paul

Medical Defence Union Annual Report (1982) quoted in The Guardian, 21st September 1983

Oswin, M. (1982), "Scenes from Ward 7" in Booth, T. and Statham, J. (eds) (1982), 306-18

Pheby, D. F. H. (1982), "Changing Practice on Confidentiality: A Cause for Concern", Journal of Medical Ethics 8 12-24

Philp, M. and Duckworth, D. (1982), Children with Disabilities and their Families: A Review of Research, Windsor: NFER-Nelson

Record, R. G. and Armstrong, E. (1975), "The influence of the birth of a malformed child on the mother's future reproduction", British Journal of Preventative and Social Medicine 29 267-73

Reid, K. (1979), Whose Children?: the interface of medical, social and educational facilities for ESN(S) children and their families in one county area in South Wales, Porthcawl Spastics Aid Group

Schrag, P. and Divoky, D. (1981), The Myth of the Hyperactive Child and Other Means of Child Control, Harmondsworth: Penguin

Stacey, M., Dearden, R., Pill, R. and Robinson, D. (1970), Hospitals, Children and their Families, London: Routledge and Kegan Paul

Stacey, M. (1980), "Charisma, Power and Altruism" in Sociology of Health and Illness 2 (1) 64-90

Stimson, G. and Webb, B. (1975), Going to See the Doctor, London: Routledge and Kegan Paul

Strong, P. M. (1979), The Ceremonial Order of the Clinic: Patients, Doctors and Medical Bureaucracies, London: Routledge and Kegan Paul

Tomlinson, S. (1982), The Sociology of Special Education, London: Routledge and Kegan Paul

Voysey, M. (1975), A Constant Burden: the reconstitution of family life, London: Routledge and Kegan Paul

Waitzkin, H. and Stoeckle, J. (1972), "The Communication of Information about Illness: clinical, sociological and methodological consideration", Advances in Psychosomatic Medicine 8 180-215

Wilkin, D. (1979), Caring for the Mentally-Handicapped Child, London: Croom Helm

INDEX

abbreviations 24
alternatives, lack of
88-90
assessment 205-6
at home 91-3
frequency of 83
hospital 62-7, 86-7, 91,
95, 113-15, 198-9
psychologist's view of
17
recalls, consulting
parents on 198-9
recommendations not
followed up 76
attendance allowance
134-5, 137, 161, 195,
210

benefits, loss of 137
bureaucracy 217-18

Campaign for People with
Mental Handicaps
190-1
Cartwright, A. 33-4, 44-5,
56, 64, 109, 112, 155,
164, 195, 217
and Anderson, R. 45,
104, 166

case-conferences 129, 220
parents' exclusion from
183-5, 203-5
cerebral palsy 190, 208
Child Poverty Action Group
191
Children's Legal Centre
191
choice, by mentally-handicapped child 173
class inequality 5
clinical medical officers
63, 65
clinics 23, 196-8, 220
recall to 105, 206
waiting times at 9-10,
23
Cohen, R. 181
collective action by
parents 4
communication 27, 32, 38,
41, 67
community care, funds for
68
community hospital 87-8,
95, 113-14
conservatism, political 99
Conservative Government
174, 211
contraception advice 199

229

Index

Davis, A. 3, 41, 93, 117,
    186-8
Davis, F. 60, 100
decision-making 103, 105-6,
    117-18, 124, 154, 177-8,
    212
diagnosis 141-2, 150-1
    information for parents
    157-8, 168
disability, physical and
    mental 189
doctor-client relations,
    interactionist studies 3
doctors
    administrative duties 63
    children underestimated
    by 85
    defensive attitude 163-5
    information given by
    138-53, 158-61, 199-201
    judgement of parents by
    148
    listening to parents
    194-7
    mistakes by 97
    not listening to parents
    71-2
    referral to other
    services by 75-7, 82,
    94, 195
    social workers and 210
    use of information from
    parents 185-8
    withholding information
    135-6
Down's Association 80, 103,
    110-11, 189
Down's Syndrome 142
drugs 133, 142, 149, 168
Dyson, S.M. 6

education
    appeals procedure 176
    government's attitude
    174
    1980 White Paper
    211-12
    mainstream 106,
    107-8
    politics and 216-17
    segregation in 211-16
Education Acts 36, 175,
    211-13, 215-16
educational psychologists
    74-7, 97-8, 115, 118,
    153-5, 162, 167, 178,
    207, 220
Educationally Sub-Normal
    (Severe) school (East
    Midlands) 6-7, 183
employment, effects on 29,
    32-3
ESN(S) schools 6-7, 84,
    115-17
    alternatives to 89-90
    appreciation of 79-80
    criteria for admission
    98, 111-12, 182-3
    decisions to admit to
    177-8, 182
    teachers at 208-9

family, handicapped 58,
    169
Family Focus 171
father's occupation 225
feeding problems 28, 47
fieldwork diary 7-8, 22
files 219-20
    access to 20, 164, 170,
    201
        parents' permission
        for 20
    closed to parents 13,
    15, 56, 70, 114, 128,
    178-81
    language of 180-1
    open 181, 201-2
Foucault (1979) 3
Fox, L. 195

genetic counselling 137,
199
Goffman, E. 209
GPs
information from 72
lack of knowledge 85
listening to parents
194-6
negative attitude 83
referrals to other
services by 75-7, 82,
195
referring child back
to 10
Griffiths Developmental
Test 138
groups for the mentally-
handicapped 189-91
see also parents groups

Hannam, C. 4, 200
health of parents 29
health visitors 76, 82, 85
information from 72
hearing problems 32, 48-9,
143-4
holidays of parents 30
hospitals
attendance at 30-1
long-stay 12-13, 67-8,
86-7, 99
phased-care in 62-3, 66,
86-8, 114, 209-10
reactions against 85
see also assessment,
hospital; community
hospital
house alterations 31

incontinence 28, 33-4, 37,
42-3, 155
information from parents,
use made of 185-8
information for parents 72,
156-7, 170, 199-201

contradictory 131
controversial 140
incorrect 130-1, 157
lack of 73-5, 102, 111,
127-30, 131-3, 160-1,
167, 169
persuasive 165-6
professional knowledge
and 138-43
on services 165-6
unhelpful 133, 142
unnecessary 152
withheld intentionally
134-8
injury, non-accidental 204
insensitiveness 10, 83-4,
135, 168, 206
interviews with parents 7,
21-2, 26-33, 146
checklist 223-4
letter requesting 222
interviews with professionals 8

Johnson, T. 217

Mayer, J. and Timms, N.
161, 210
Medical Defence Union
97-8
medical knowledge 91
medical officers 207
MENCAP 80, 189, 190
mental handicap, mild and
severe 189
mentally-handicapped
definition 7
marginal to professionals'
work 11
MIND 190
mobility of children 26-7,
32
moral judgements 55-6,
58-9, 68, 84, 154
mother

extra work expected of
43, 52, 54-5, 58, 68
paid employment of 59,
69
relatives' help for 58,
209-10

National Association for
the Welfare of Children
in Hospital 191
National Council for Civil
Liberties 191
nurses 82, 85

occupational therapy 77-8
one-parent families 54-5,
69, 100, 190
Oswin, M. 66

paediatricians 206
clinics 197-8
listening to parents
195-7
parent's dissatisfaction
with junior 206-7
parent/professional
relations, management
of 60-8, 108-18, 156-65
parents
access to files 201
denied 178-81
advice to 57, 82, 88-90,
106
aid for 70
case-conferences and
203-5
communication with 16
consulting on assess-
ments 198
criticism of profess-
ionals 2-3, 13, 97, 156
decision-making and
103, 105-6, 117-18, 124,
154, 212

employment 29, 225
exclusion from case
conferences 183-5
extra work expected of
51-7, 59, 68-9
files closed to 13, 15,
56, 70, 114, 128, 178-81
groups 70, 77, 103-4,
136, 145, 171, 188-9,
210
health 29
interviews with 7, 21-2,
26-33, 146, 222-4
judging appropriateness
of 18-20
knowledge needed by
171, 175-8
listening to 194-7
losses in using services
125
moral judgements on
55-6, 58-9, 68, 84, 154
not listened to 71-2, 90,
104, 136, 196
partnership with
professionals 171-5
permission to use files
14-16
problems 9-10
professionals'
attitude 10, 39, 41,
45-9, 100
expectations 51-6,
59, 102-8, 151-6
power over 13, 15,
115-17, 125, 169,
172, 177, 183, 185
views on 180-2
reassuring 145-6, 162
rejection of services by
105-6, 118-19, 124-5
report for 23-4
rights of 155, 175, 177
time and energy wasted
80, 82-3, 90

unhelpful services
offered to 62-7, 69, 70
use made of informa-
tion from 185-8
see also father; infor-
mation for parents;
mother; partnership
Parkinson's Disease 190
partnership, parent/
professional 171-2
involving child in
172-5
phased-care 62-3, 66, 86-8,
114, 209-10
Pheby, D.F.H. 205
Phenytoin 149
Philp, M. and Duckworth,
D. 4, 86-7, 199
physiotherapy 78-9, 91,
98, 121-3, 155
value of 208
professional files see
files
professional knowledge
33-5, 42-4, 90-4
information for parents
and 138-43
lack of action on 35-41
limits to 44-51, 95-103,
143-51, 158, 168, 184
provided by parents
143-4
professional routines 80-2
professional/parent partnership 171-2
involving child in 172-5
professonal/parent rela-
tions, management of
60-8, 108-18, 156-65
professionals
advice to parents 57
attitude to parents 10,
39, 41, 45-9, 100
community-based 198-9
differences in dealing

with problems 42
disagreements between
202-3
expectations of parents
51-6, 59, 102-8, 151-6
information from see
information for parents
insensitiveness 10, 83-4,
168, 206
interviews with 8
listening to parents
194-7
mentally-handicapped
marginal to work of 11
moral judgements 55-6,
58-9, 68, 94, 154
numbers at clinics 10
parents' criticism of
2-3, 13, 97, 156
patronizing 115
politically conserv-
ative 99
power over parents 13,
15, 115-17, 125, 169,
172, 177, 183, 185
relations between
17-18, 64-6, 69, 81,
98-9, 112, 118-23, 125
management of 165-7
report for 23-4
roles and procedures of
175-8
self-protection 1, 3, 65,
108, 110-13, 118-19,
165
social judgements 68-9
stereotyping by 11-12,
100, 113, 116, 125
underestimation of
mentally-handicapped
94
views on parents 180-2
psychologists
assessment consultant's
view of 17

criticism of teachers 17
educational 74-7, 97-8,
115, 118, 153-5, 162,
167, 178, 207, 220
files 13

racial inequality 5
Record, R.G. and
Armstrong, E. 199
records 91, 94, 115
destruction of 3
required of doctors 39
referral to other services
75-7, 82, 94, 120, 195,
207
Reid, K. 4
research 4, 219-21
respite-care see phased-
care
reviews of literature 1-2

sample of children 21, 219
Schrag, P. and Divoky, D.
13, 133, 179
segregation
educational 211-16
social 99
versus integration
173-4, 215-16
self-protection, profess-
ionals' 1, 3, 65, 108,
110-13, 118-19, 165
services
inappropriate 86-8,
105-6, 109
information on 165-6
lack of most helpful
77-80
parental losses in
using 125
parents' rights to 112
referral to other 75-7,
82, 94, 120, 195, 207
rejected by parents 115,
118-19, 124-5

use of, stigmatizing
parents 100
voluntary 80
sex inequality 5
shared-care see phased-
care
single-parent family see
one-parent family
sleeplessness 27
social judgements 68-9, 151
social services
access to files 7
parents' criticism of 19
social workers 16, 74, 88,
100-1, 127-8, 210-11
cases not referred to 77
team of 11
sociology, professionals'
view of 12
sources of data 6-8
special equipment 31-3
special schools 13-14,
89-90, 94, 207
admission to 36-7
segregation in 213
see also ESN(S) schools
speech therapy 78
Stacey, M. 135, 194-5
et al. 30
stereotyping 11-12, 100,
113, 116, 125
Stimson, G. and Webb, B.
3, 45, 47, 104, 108,
111, 118, 142, 148, 151
154, 157, 159, 161
developing 35, 39, 57,
91, 113
Strong, P.M. 3
symbols 25

taxation of minorities 174
teachers, professionals'
criticism of 17-18
therapists, referral to 207
Tomlinson, S. 214

Index

trade unions 191
transport problems 28, 31,
    60

voluntary services 80

waiting times 9-10, 23, 81
Whyte, William Foote 5
Wilkin, D. 21, 210